Teaching with Comedy

A Guide for Using
Humor in the Classroom

EVAN HOOVLER

750
PUBLISHING

To my mother, Judy

© 2019 Evan Hoovler

Published by Kaplan Publishing
750 Third Avenue
New York, NY 10017

All rights reserved. The text of this publication, or any part thereof, may not be reproduced in any manner whatsoever without written permission of the publisher.

10 9 8 7 6 5 4 3 2 1

ISBN: 978-1-5062-5814-0

TABLE OF CONTENTS

CHAPTER 1: A HISTORY OF USING COMEDY TO INCREASE STUDENT RETENTION
    Comedy of Ancient History........................1
    Comedy of the Middle Ages and the Renaissance.......15
    Comedy of Early America 19
    Comedy of the Post-Civil War Era................. 24

CHAPTER 2: JOKEMAKING TECHNIQUES WORKBOOK
    Reading Your Target Audience...................... 29
    Formula 1: Schlemiel-Schlimazel................... 35
    Formula 2: The Forced Transition..................... 42
    Formula 3: The 1-2-3 44
    Formula 4: Exaggeration 55
    Formula 5: Repetition 72
    Formula 6: Personification........................ 87
    Formula 7: The Grand Opening 90

CHAPTER 3: COMMON JOKEMAKING TRAPS
    Jokemaking Trap 1: Telegraphing 111
    Jokemaking Trap 2: Reference Comedy................ 118
    Jokemaking Trap 3: Taking Too Long 119
    Jokemaking Trap 4: Puns and Wordplay 122
    Jokemaking Trap 5: Embracing Bad Comedy..........128
    Jokemaking Trap 6: Monkeycheese................... 131
    Jokemaking Trap 7: Worrying about the Stalwarts 140

CONCLUSION...143
ENDNOTES 144
ART CREDITS.......................................146

CHAPTER 1
A HISTORY OF USING COMEDY TO INCREASE STUDENT RETENTION

Comedy of Ancient History

The link between comedy and increased learning has a long and storied history. It dates back, perhaps, to the first teachers ever. And who is the most famous ancient teacher? Plato, of course. Check out what this zany educator had to say about combining teaching and comedy:

> *For ordinarily when one abandons himself to violent laughter, his condition provokes a violent reaction. If anyone represents men of worth as overpowered by laughter we must not accept it, much less if gods.*[1]

Well, that wasn't quite the ringing endorsement I was looking for to open this book. I'm sure it was just a rare moment where Plato didn't say something glowing about comedy. Let's dig up another quote:

> *In laughing...we take delight in something evil—their self-ignorance—and that malice is morally objectionable.*[2]

Fine! Okay, fine, Plato, you're a humorless jerk! Anything else you want to add, or are you finished utterly butchering my book intro?

> *We shall enjoin that such representations be left to slaves or—*[3]

Seriously, Plato, shut up already. You ruin everything, including my ability to write a book while doing research on the fly.

Take a deep breath, Evan.

Okay. It looks like Plato hated comedy. Not what I expected, but I can work with that. For instance, how many of Plato's teachings can you actually recall? I can't think of any, in part because he was from a long line of humorless instructors with attitudes so arid they are the pedagogical equivalent of dying of thirst in the desert.

I laid this all out for you to illustrate the main element of using humor in the classroom: It's not about things going right. It's about celebrating when things go wrong. Students will remember that things went wrong when I tried to use the writings of Plato to promote laughter in education and, more importantly, they'll remember that ancient philosophers were pretty serious about keeping comedy and education separate. It's fascinating stuff, but if I had just presented Plato's meandering, archaic quotes, I guarantee my class's eyeballs would glaze over like a box of donuts. So would your eyeballs. So would your wallets when you decide whether to buy this book. Stop keeping eyeballs in your wallets.

Part of the reason why Plato's stodgy views on comedy persisted for so long was because they happened thousands of years before we got really good at science. Science shows that his views on comedy are, frankly, wrong: humor, when effectively delivered, does increase retention. Let's hammer home how much humor helps learning with a staple of modern comedy: rigidly conducted academic studies!

A study conducted within the last 10 years (in other words: 9 years ago) surveyed hundreds of college students about what types of humor increased retention. Not surprisingly, appropriate and relevant humor was positively correlated with higher learning retention. Inappropriate or off-topic humor saw no correlation.

This is a key point that I will be returning to constantly throughout this book: it's just as important to know when *not* to use humor as it is to know when to use humor. The survey, titled "An Explanation of the Relationship between Instructor Humor and Student Learning: Instructional Humor Processing Theory,"[4] illustrates the fine line one must walk when deciding whether or not to use humor.

No wonder Plato's name became the basis for the word *platonic*, which means "Nobody wants an intimate relationship with you."

To wit: if one uses relevant, acceptable humor, then learning will increase. For example: "If there's anyone who knows about humor, it's the scientists dull enough to title their study 'An Explanation of the Relationship between Instructor Humor and Student Learning: Instructional Humor Processing Theory.'" If one uses inappropriate or off-topic humor, then learning won't increase.

I can show this by asking you to recite the title of the study we're talking about. I bet you can't because my joke was mean. So stop making fun of scientists, everyone, or we'll never be able to remember what they're teaching us.

Now, we shouldn't ignore the shortcoming of this study, which is that there was no testing done to prove retention was increased; it relied solely on the students reporting whether or not they increased learning. Also, the categories of appropriate and inappropriate humor can also be called into question, as most people tend to define *appropriate* as "it made me laugh."

Here's another key takeaway from the study:

Humor can be perceived and appreciated without improving retention—essentially, the student can think a teacher is funny but not show an improvement in retention. **So just being silly may get your students' attention, but it may not lead to better retention.** These researchers concluded that topical, appropriate, and instructional humor is most effective for increasing retention.

So just using wacky humor irrelevant to the situation, or as scientists call it, "monkeycheesing," doesn't increase student retention.

This is a sore point for me, as a lot of material out there promotes silly behavior, such as a National Education Association paper on effective teaching, which advocates "taking roll in an English accent, tap dancing on the desk, singing the answers to a test."[5]

Getting back to that study, I know what you're all saying: "Evan, I have a PhD in sociology, and I have questions about the methodology of this examination." You're right: simply having students report whether funny teachers increased learning is open to bias. After all, students learn more from teachers they like, and people tend to laugh more at the jokes of people they like. So we may have a correlation-doesn't-equal-causation situation here, where both the laughter and the increased retention are independently caused by a separate factor.

While you're all lining up to second-guess me, let me note that comedy today is much broader than in Plato's time. According to scholars (I'll cite one so this statement looks super official), Greek comedy at the time of the great philosophers was "bawdy and ribald songs or recitations apropos of phallic processions and fertility festivals or gatherings."[6]

The first thing I took from this is that "fertility festival" used to have a much dirtier meaning, making me question the morality of Easter eggs. But the main thing I took from it is that there was probably a different reason Plato wanted to keep comedy out of schools: obscenity has no place in any classroom.

Still, this does not undermine my point: humor increases retention. I guarantee that if I tried to teach a math formula with a limerick that started, "There once was a man from Cnidus, he had a pencil with girth enormous…," you'd for sure remember whatever formula was being demonstrated (probably πr^2; Greeks love πr^2).

Other Greek philosophers around their time had a less strict regard for the merging of the humorous and the important. Aristotle considered comedy to be a cornerstone of literature and a fundamental reflection of real life.[7] I trust his view more than Plato's, and not just because he is supporting my fundamental point. Unlike Plato's horrid moniker *platonic*, Aristotle's name was used to form the word *aristocrats*, which means "people in charge." Checkmate: Aristotle equals right and in charge, Plato equals wrong and loveless.

Aristotle also had a much more progressive view on humor than his fellow b.c.e. philosophers. He had the avant-garde notion that jokes could be, like, funny and stuff and that humor could have a net benefit on society. He also advocated that comedy didn't have to involve crude sexual humor, despite that Greek fashion meant everyone was constantly under a bedsheet. He argues that comedy could bring forth happiness, which for him was the ideal state of life.

For me, the ideal state of life is "alive," but Aristotle's theories do mean something to me.

Because there were so many warring city-states in Ancient Greece, gang insignias had to be a lot more detailed.

You see, I got into comedy at a young age because I realized that everybody dies and there's a not-insignificant chance that life is a meaningless husk in the void of the universe. Look, I know it's grim, but that's what happens to youth when the 1980s-era NBC TV network airs *Cheers* (a show about alcoholics) and *Dear John* (a show about a depressed divorcée) directly after the family-friendly hit *The Cosby Show*.

I got that ennui early. I learned that the only surefire way out of this emotional sinkhole was through laughter, and soon learned that a properly placed joke can shake anyone from the clutches of grief, however briefly.

When I got into teaching, I realized the similar power of laughter, for what's the only thing worse than the meaninglessness of existence? That's right, math word problems.

So I started trying the power of humor in my classes. Not a lot mind you; just like a grieving widow doesn't want to hear an entire stand-up set, a geometry class doesn't want to hear their teacher use them as a captive audience at an open mic. But I soon found that the right, carefully positioned joke could shake them from the tedious purgatory of standardized education.

Back to the Greeks. If we really want to get to the ultimate root, the patient zero of infectious laughter, we need to take a look at Aristophanes. Aristophanes wrote comedic plays still studied today, and his name is the root of the word *aristophats*, which sounds like *aristocrats*, so you can rest assured I've vetted him with our foolproof litmus test and determined him to be good.

I know what you're thinking: "Evan, do I really have to learn about Ancient Greek plays just to engage my class? I've never felt more disengaged than when you wrote, 'Hey, let's look at some Greek plays!'"

My response is as simple as it is aggressive. First, I never said, "Hey, let's look at some Greek plays," and I don't appreciate you misquoting me, dear reader. Second, that's the whole point of me picking Greek plays: to bore you. I'm teaching by example here, and to do so I must first put you into the mindset of a bored student. So pay attention to the ways I get you interested, or at least focused, on the Ancient Greek playwright who is the root of modern comedy.

See what I did there? I took the fact that I am a boring writer with a tedious subject and made it sound super important through comedy. That's what we do here.

Back to Aristophanes. He's known as the Father of Comedy. Yeah, he's that important. He wrote 40 plays, over a quarter of which were considered so important that they were preserved in their entirety for 2,500 years.

You know what else he did?

He killed Socrates. More on that later.

What made Aristophanes so well regarded in Ancient Greece, besides his dislike for Socrates, was that he was really, really funny for his time and wasn't afraid to skewer those in charge. What makes him so well regarded for the purposes of this book is that he is the first person we can find who used comedy for teaching.

See, Greek plays often have something called a *chorus*, a group of people who come out and comment on the play. It's useful for explaining complicated things and making the play more relatable. I wish it was used by Shakespeare because I could never understand his ancient English rapping or whatever it's supposed to be. A Greek chorus was used by Aristophanes to provide his own biting commentary and to educate the crowds as to the issues he felt were important.

In the comedy biz, "he killed Socrates" is what's known as a tease: a short preview of an interesting part of the lesson coming up later. It wakes up sleepy audiences and keeps them leaning forward through the more rote learning part of the lesson. Students will pay attention to me droning on about ancient plays because they won't want to miss the part where I explain how Aristophanes killed Socrates. Hopefully, you will too.

For instance, there was a prominent leader at the time known as Cleon. I looked him up on my smartphone. Once it stopped asking me if I had misspelled "Klingon," it told me that Cleon hated Aristophanes's portrayal of the police in his second play. Now, whether or not Aristophanes was sent to trial for this is a matter of debate, but what we all know for sure is that, from that point on, Aristophanes started regularly including a character in his plays that represented Cleon as a bumbling, corrupt, violent idiot. It turns out people really dig offensive political satire, a concept that continues today in the form of news parodies such as *SNL*, *The Daily Show*, and 95 percent of the content on 24-hour news channels.

Now, you may be asking yourself, "How does this directly relate to teaching with comedy? Insulting public figures may be hilarious, but I can't really do that in class, Mr. Stupid Comedy Book Guy."

I can work with that. I love an assertive audience.

I can also work with an apathetic audience, but there's only so many times I can respond to an email that asks, "Mr. Hoovler, what can I do to bring my grade up?" with "You can do the homework. Literally any of the homework that I've assigned. Ever. Something, anything, just do anything! That's what you can do! Before I lose my mind."

So I like people who care about bettering themselves. I like you.

In the days before comedy news shows, nobody remembered anything. This is why it's so hard to piece together ancient history.

For example: The other day a student vocally complained about her workload and even stated, "If I have all this extra stuff to learn outside of class, are you even doing your job?" The class chuckled and murmured, a prime situation for using humor to get things back on track.

I responded, "I like your negativity and your assertiveness. Honestly, I love negativity and assertiveness. That may seem weird, but if you don't believe me you can ask my wife...who will say I definitely *don't* love negativity and assertiveness. Because she's negative and assertive, and that's why I love her." Bond established, I then told the now-attentive student some ways to keep on top of her workload.

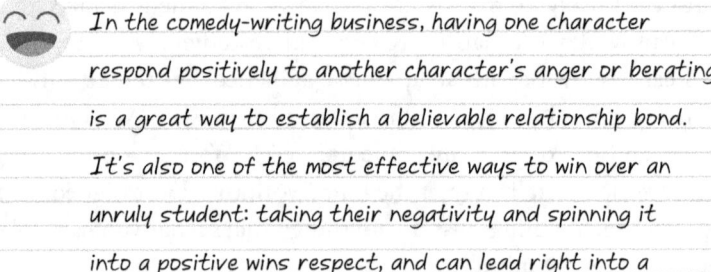

> In the comedy-writing business, having one character respond positively to another character's anger or berating is a great way to establish a believable relationship bond. It's also one of the most effective ways to win over an unruly student: taking their negativity and spinning it into a positive wins respect, and can lead right into a humorous anecdote.

So the whole point of my telling you about Aristophanes's legendary political wit is to reinforce that the key to comedy is steering into the unexpected. Aristophanes made some satirical comments about the police, and the next thing he knew, he was being called out by an extremely powerful and unstable figure. Aristophanes (did he have a nickname, by the way? I'm getting really sick of typing *Aristophanes*) didn't cower away, he didn't switch careers into farming or whatever the other job was back then. He saw a crazy despot throwing his weight around obnoxiously and said…

"I can work with that."

At this point in my lecturing, people often stop me and say, "Hey, man," or, if they know my name, "Hey, Evan, if the key to class retention is to harness the unexpected, how am I supposed to learn and practice your jokes ahead of time?"

It's simple: you're not.

I'm not writing this book to teach you how to become the world's best comedian, to have classes doubling over with laughter over your prudently crafted takes on the human condition. If that's what you want, buy a book from a more famous comedian.

I'm writing this book to give you the tools to steer a distracted class back to focusing on the lesson at hand. To get them to pay attention when you've got a batch of less-than-succulent facts to shove up their brains. The way to do that is with a decently crafted joke.

Science backs me up when it comes to humor and knowledge retention: A study titled "The Effect of Humor on Retention of Learning Material"[8] was conducted on students at California State University at Dominguez Hills. This was in 1981, back when we couldn't effortlessly Google "how to be a funny teacher" and get a bunch of utterly incorrect advice. At this point in time, science was divided as to whether humor had any place as a teaching aid. This study wanted to settle the raging (and probably humorless) debate on whether laughter had a role in the classroom.

Specifically, the goals were to make sure the funny bits that were presented to test subjects were actually perceived as funny by the test takers and to see if it mattered whether the humor was related to the material. The study's administrators were named Desberg, Henschel, Marshall, and McGhee. I'm not sure what you're supposed to do with that information, but I feel like I'm supposed to say the names of the people who made the studies I cite so they can feel famous or something.

Back to the point. The study presented to subjects a videotaped (yeah, it's that old) lecture on language development. Each student saw the same lecture with a tweak in one of four different ways:

1. One group had a nonhumorous lecture.
2. One group had a lecture with humor unrelated to the subject matter.
3. One group had a lecture with humor related to the subject matter.
4. One group had no humor, but points were repeated at the places where jokes were in the humorous lectures. This was to test if an increase in retention was just due to repeating the info in a joke, and not the joke itself.

Afterward, the subjects were given a test. These test answers were analyzed and it was determined that the lecture with related humor increased retention more than the no-humor or unrelated humor lecture.

So there it is: humor helps increase learning retention. It's science. You can't argue with it.

"But, Evan," you might argue, "you didn't include the fourth lecture style. What about the people who didn't have a lecture with humor, but did see the lecture that repeated concepts as much as the related humor lecture?"

Well, I might reply to that question with a question. I might ask, "Did you really just buy this book to argue with me every step of the way?" I might ask, "Why is one of the author's names misspelled on the title page of this study?" (It really is. Google it.) That's not really relevant, but since we're talking about boring old studies, I wanted to insert some humor to increase retention, even though we haven't actually established that it works.

What is relevant are the results of the fourth lecture, where they tested whether just repeating the information without humor was effective. Listen up, all you humor doubters, the study clearly says that... hold on let me scroll down... here it is:

Because the related humor condition and the repetition control condition did not differ in retention, it may be assumed that these two conditions served the same purpose of verbally underlining the fact to be learned.[9]

See? Stick that in your pipe and clog it. Or, wait... actually that said the opposite of what I wanted it to. Apparently, just repeating something is what makes people learn more, not the humor itself.

Okay... I can work with that.

Because the main purpose of humor is to celebrate the unexpected. So whenever I make a mistake, it's a teaching moment. It's also a moment to pretend like I intentionally made the mistake so no one knows how epically bad I am at simple things like reading comprehension.

Pretend you didn't read that last sentence and let me explain why I completely intentionally chose a study that says humor is no better at increasing retention than simple repetition.

The key to increasing retention with humor is to use it sparingly. Information doesn't need a joke attached to it to be retained. No one thinks, "Aww, what was my mom's phone number? If only she had included it in a dirty limerick, then I'd remember."

That's a serious point I will be revisiting many times: don't force in humor if the class is already paying attention. A motivated, calm class will remember just as much through humorous repetition as it will through humorless repetition. There's no need to treat each lecture like open microphone night at the comedy club...although the way educational funding is decreasing, we might have to require each class to have a two-drink minimum.

Because humor shouldn't be forced, it also shouldn't be rehearsed. It's best used to get a distracted class back on track or to keep things moving when a teacher makes a mistake like forgetting a decimal, or forgetting an apostrophe, or forgetting the results of a 1981 study that they skimmed before writing a monumentally important book about comedy and teaching.

Speaking of that study, it goes on to conclude: "Subjects basically found the related humor lecture more humorous than the repetition control lecture...Furthermore, subjects report finding the humorous presentation more enjoyable. Therefore, in cases of rote learning, related jokes contribute by both repeating and concept and making the learning process more enjoyable."

That actually has a subtle long-term effect on retention. If students find a lecture more enjoyable, they are going to come into the next lecture motivated to learn.

The important thing to take from this whole thing is that there is definitely room for humor in teaching—and that when I start detailing a boring study you should pay attention on the off chance the whole thing turns into a fascinating train wreck.

Getting Greek again, Aristotle was one of the first to note that screwing up gracefully presents ample opportunity. In his words,

"An ugliness that does not disgust is fundamental to humor." We're not here to gain the admiration of our class. Spoiler alert: many students don't want to be in class and are going to resent us no matter what we do—even the kindergarteners, who never want to be wherever they currently are (mostly because that would involve staying still).

Okay, maybe not all the kindergarteners. But definitely the woke six-year-old ones. Speaking of kindergarteners, it's important we don't apply the results of studies and surveys aimed at college students to little children because little children have it way more together than the average college student.

A study of humor and retention for kindergarteners and first graders was conducted in 1980.[10] I don't know what it was about 1980 that made researchers so obsessed with humor and learning. Maybe it was the constant threat of nuclear war, or maybe it was the defunding of mental hospitals so we comedians were forced to roam the public streets.

Whatever it was, it inspired D. Zillmann, B. R. Williams, J. Bryant, K. R. Boynton, and M. A. Wolf to study how well young students remember information presented to them via sketches from *Sesame Street*.

In this study, kindergarteners and first graders were given one of five *Sesame Street* clips:

1. Humorous segments interspersed with educational learning
2. The same humorous segments, but shown more frequently in between the educational learning parts
3. No humorous inserts
4. Serious inserts
5. Serious inserts paced quickly

The study found that the clips with humorous segments were the ones students were more likely to recall and demonstrate learning from.

You might be wondering, "Hey, why are all your studies from 40 years ago?" to which I politely say, "Look, you want me to go over Plato and Aristotle some more?" Of course not—you want something more modern, more accessible than Plato and Aristotle.

Let's look at 600 years ago.

Comedy of the Middle Ages and the Renaissance

Education and comedy, at least as we've come to think of it in the Western world, didn't change much in the transition from the Greeks to the Romans. It wasn't until the Age of Enlightenment that people began to view humor in new ways. Gone were the stodgy, unyielding views of comedy from Stone Age philosophers. No more would education be in the hands of a few powerful (and extremely humorless) individuals. The future of the world's pupils was now firmly in the control of the no-doubt easygoing and open-minded—hold on, let me look up who it was...

> *The increasing influence of Church became the guiding force to develop educational systems in The Middle Ages.*[11]

Oh. I did not expect that.

That's okay, I can work with that.

That's what's so exciting about modern theory toward educational methods: we have such new ideas about the retentive powers of humor that are just now being explored. Teachers in the 1400s had no idea that combining news with humor, like in *The Daily Show*, would be scientifically shown to create more knowledgeable students. I referenced *The Daily Show*, so I'm linking in modern elements! Is that show still on?

A 2007 research poll found that people who watch comedy news shows such as *The Daily Show* and *The Colbert Report* showed a higher retention than people who got their news from CNN or other nonhumorous TV news programs.[12] The study also said that people who watched comedy news shows retained more info than people who got their news from newspapers, but I'm throwing out that fact. I don't think it's fair to use a TV show versus newspaper comparison as evidence that one has a higher likelihood to educate because it could just be that the average newspaper reader is, like, 70 years old and has trouble retaining information about everything.

Note: If I offended any septuagenarian newspaper readers, I apologize. Thank you for buying this book, and please don't let my flippant quip stop you from recommending this book to other newspaper readers, most of whom will no doubt be interested to know that it also comes in a large print edition.

The point still stands that we live in an exciting, connected world that presents novel opportunity to use humor to increase learning retention in ways never before thought possible. Certainly not by the educators and humorists of the Renaissance period, who were definitely not keen on mixing the two. The church's consideration of the arts in education was so minor that any student who could prove that they "knew" arts was announced as a master of arts, often needing to show little more than how to write their numbers and name. I had a similar experience getting my master's degree in arts, mainly because writing numbers and my name is all I needed to give the school a check every year.

This isn't meant to paint the church as explicitly working to outlaw humor; it's simply the nature of humor that made it incongruent with the educational system established by the church.

So while education may have gotten even more narrow-minded in the caste-structured Middle Ages, humor certainly should have evolved, right? After all, the concepts of mirth and introspection were no longer reserved for navel-gazing philosophers and apple-gazing gravitational scientists.

A History of Using Comedy to Increase Student Retention | 17

Comedy in church could have gotten more people into spirituality if they required a two-communion minimum.

Well, it's not so much that humor evolved a great degree during this time as it is that humor became much more common. It was during this period that some of the first stand-up comedians emerged: court jesters. Their humor was not so much evolved as it was particularly honed for their target audience (see chapter 2 for more about target audience). In the Middle Ages, unfortunately, their target audience was usually the nobleman who employed them and had little perspective on the struggles of commoners. As such, most jesters' jokes were limited to self-deprecating slapstick and derisive impressions of their employer's enemies. Today, our modern politicians have figured out they can do self-deprecating slapstick just by being themselves.

Although this history lesson is set hundreds of years ago, it does have a prominent parallel that applies to modern times: when those who have the most access to studying comedy are not themselves well versed in what qualifies as good comedy, the quality of humor suffers. Therefore, retention suffers.

As for the "commoners' comedians," they were there. A lot of tongue-in-cheek jokes were made about the hypocrisy between the perfectionistic standards required of serfs by the church and the fact that humans are imperfect creatures. This is why it's difficult to understand the zeitgeist, or cultural view, of humor in the Renaissance. The most popular forms of humor involved poking fun directly at the institution that controlled the schools, which meant that education would never be able to incorporate humor.

That's also why a history of comedy is so murky to write about. Also, because nobody could write jokes down back then due to illiteracy.

Fortunately, the fields of entertainment and education weren't completely separate. John Amos Comenius was a bishop who lived during the 17th century. He championed education for all and came up with ways to make learning much more engaging and fun. He is often referred to as the father of modern education.

The Renaissance was not just the end of the Dark Ages in terms of science and reasoning. It also showed the first signs that education did not have to be completely boring. To put in perspective exactly how boring education was in the 1600s, one of the "revolutionary" ideas Comenius had was, "Hey, you know what might make this informative text a bit less mind-achingly dull? Some pictures!" Explanatory illustrations were unheard of before then. Well, not totally unheard of because there were, you know, hieroglyphics… but the concept of combining school texts with pictures was unheard of.

Comenius put forth that maybe the best way for someone to learn was not by rote memorization of texts, presumably while whipping oneself (because my entire research into this area was done by reading the *Da Vinci Code*). He wanted to bring elements into education to make it more practical and, dare he say it, entertaining.

Comenius's influence was widespread. It was a pretty easy sell to say, "Hey, I might have a better way to teach you besides sitting in a dusty room reading a dusty Bible." (There was a lot of dust back in the Renaissance.)

Comenius would have probably done even more for the field of edutainment had his efforts not seen a few failed starts. He was even given the task of reforming England's education system, a chore that might have put Western comedy and education centuries beyond where it is now. However, the one thing humans love more than laughing is killing each other, and a civil war put the kibosh on Comenius's progress.

He was a genius ahead of his time. And as would usually happen to geniuses who were ahead of their time, he was quickly excommunicated and became a religious refugee.

Comedy of Early America

Comenius founded edutainment, and Ben Franklin brought it to America. Benjamin "Mr. Franklin" Franklin published a wildly successful pamphlet called *Poor Richard's Almanack*. The almanac combined factual elements with fun ones, usually featuring weather forecasts and quizzes.

Commodities were scarce in the New World during the 1700s (which is why people considered quizzes to be "fun"). So Benjamin Franklin wasn't publishing these almanacs as a community service. He needed to sell them, and that meant putting in more than just a weather outlook and a puzzle. Otherwise, people could just ask their neighbors, "Hey, what is the weather going to be like?" Or, since this was New England, people could just carve "really, really bad" onto a tree and go look at it every time they wondered what the weather would be like.

The difficult conditions led Franklin to realize that some mirth would be quite marketable as a portion of his book. So he started putting in quips, sayings, and incredibly bizarre-yet-funny cliffhangers. One of the most famous of these concerned a fictional character, Leeds, who was predicted to die on October 17. Leeds was outraged at this prediction, insisting that he would die on October 26. That's pretty funny, albeit morbid. What's interesting is, presumably due to the lack of anything better to do, people actually waited a year to buy the next almanac and find out if Leeds did in fact die on October 17 or 26. That's weird. But what's even weirder is that Ben Franklin kept the ruse going for another year by not revealing the death date. Historians really can't tell if this was actually a riveting plot or if Franklin was dropping a satirical tease to ensure his captive audience would stay focused on buying his almanacs. Either way, the bottom line is that Ben Franklin had figured out a way to make money by combining humor with education, even if they were only linked by being contained in the same book.

Naturally, the leaps in educational entertainment mirrored the leaps in entertainment technology. With television and movies came a much easier way to make entertaining-yet-informative programming. Naturally, it should come as no surprise that pushing the frontiers of this field was one of the most entertaining entities on earth: the US Army.

Wait, no that can't be right. But it's mostly true: it was Walt Disney who worked with the US Army during World War II to make a bunch of educational shorts. Disney knew the inherent value of bringing education to children through comedic skits, and moreover he knew the inherent value of money and that edutainment was an untouched gold mine. The first thing Disney had to do to establish an edutainment empire was invent the word *edutainment*. Then he went on to make educational shorts such as that one where Donald Duck teaches geometry by shooting billiards. That taught me a lot, but it would have saved me a lot of cash if Donald would have also taught me that someone with a custom pool cue, a lisp, and a webbed hand was not easy money in poolroom gambling.

Therein lies exactly why we live in an exciting era of new teaching opportunities. For the first time, we live in a time when all the institutions of life are sufficiently compartmentalized, from religion to education to entertainment to everything. I can make fun of a study without my target audience for this book thinking I'm utterly discrediting the value of science.

On that note, there have been more recent studies supporting the now-obvious link between humor and learning retention. However, I can't just select any study; I have to be discriminating because, frankly, some of these studies are so pedantic that I'm not sure the people involved have any idea what humor is and, in fact, might be robots. Take the seminal study, "Humor in the Home and in the Classroom: The Benefits of Laughing While We Learn."

First, I know what you're thinking. "Is this *the* 'Humor in the Home and in the Classroom: The Benefits of Laughing While We Learn'[13] that appeared in the *Journal of Education and Human Development*, volume 2, issue 1, in 2008? The same study authored by Michael G. Lovorn, PhD, Assistant Professor, California State University, Long Beach?"

To which I say, "Hold on…let me Google it…yes!"

That paper does a lot to argue that humor is an essential tool to facilitate learning. So I want to lay it all out before you as a beacon of my philosophy: that humor is an exciting and effective classroom tool to increase (when used strategically) class retention on important subjects, such as split infinitives. But it wouldn't be comedy if I didn't trip up during practically every step of this journey through time and effectively sourced research. While I was rushing through this study to cherry-pick the parts of it that best support my claims, I came across this statement:

> *According to* Webster's New World Dictionary, *to laugh means to "make the explosive sounds of the voice and the characteristic movements of the features of the body, that express mirth, amusement, ridicule, etc."* [14]

This is why I hate this study. I don't know why the author felt the need to cite experts just to say, "I looked up the definition of a word that everyone already knows." He goes on to further undermine my ability to take him seriously by adding:

> *This definition might do well to explain the physiological event of laughter, but to understand the effects it has on one's social or emotional wellbeing, more clinical definitions are necessary.* [15]

More clinical? Really? There's a level of clinical that's more intense than defining *laugh* with a double-sourced definition?

I'm not sure this obviously well-read scholar is going to be my go-to name when it comes to analyzing comedy.

Which brings in another key issue: whom can we trust when it comes to actually determining if comedy should be used in the classroom? Obviously we should respect anyone who uses words like *whom* when referring to the object of a sentence, as they sound like an expert. But how do we know if they're funny?

After all, "Everyone thinks they're funny," goes the old saying, yet hospitalization of students for eye-rolling injuries is at an all-time high. I certainly think that I'm funny: I've written comedy that has been seen by over 10 million people... and only about 9 million of those people left angry comments, so I'm feeling pretty confident in that department.

The simple answer for who determines if someone is funny is: the audience. If they laugh, it's funny. If not, even if the joke is *really good when I told it to my mom and she laughed*, it's not funny. Which is why it's so important to focus on studies like "The Effect of Humor on Retention of Learning Material," mentioned earlier, where the subjects get to rate the comedy on how funny it really was.

So when did humor shift away from some man stumbling around in brightly colored tights into something that could serve as a vehicle for more erudite thought?

The answer is George Washington.

Well, actually George Washington can't be the answer because the question was "when" and George Washington hasn't been a time since we merged his birthday into Presidents' Day. But when the United States was a fledgling nation, its leaders were already well-versed in the effective use of comedy when it came to motivating people about more serious matters.

The medieval church had a strong insistence in separating students, artists, and soldiers. Washington, however, knew from his experience as a war leader that there was much to be gained from mixing the areas together. I had mentioned I got into comedy not for the mirth, but for the salve-like properties of good jokes to heal the wounds of traumas and existential crises. Washington felt the same: his seven years as leader of the Continental Army saw prolonged fighting that took a brutal toll on his men. While Washington couldn't provide physical comfort, he could provide relief in the form of quality humor. Upon realizing that his host at a meal had made some hideous jeweled cups before becoming a minimalist Quaker preacher, Washington quipped, "I wish he'd become a preacher before he made these cups."[16]

Other quips that kept up the resolve of his troops during times of dire need include "The Army, as usual, are without Pay; and a great part of the Soldiery without Shirts; and tho' the patience of them is equally threadbare" and "Once woman has tempted us and we have tasted the forbidden fruit, there is no such thing as checking our appetites."

Well, okay, that last one had nothing to do with war. It's hard to find good one-liners from a dude from 300 years ago.

Ironically, the tough, war-stricken times of the Federalist period in American history were not ones known for the development of new methods of mirth. Or maybe they were—I must admit I don't know a lot about early 18th-century joke writing because 300-year-olds are rarely in my target audience. It's a good thing too: no matter how great my jokes are, I can never seem to get them to focus on my lesson.

So let me look this up from a reliable source. By which I mean, "Let me find something on Wikipedia, then click the footnote, then cite that as the source so you don't realize I'm just looking up things on Wikipedia." Yeah, sometimes I learn things from my students too.

Another reason why we can go ahead and gloss right through the history of comedy in the early 18th century is because it's just so offensive. The best audience is a warm audience, those relaxed and looking to laugh, and the warmest audience is by far a drunk one. That's being excessively glib, I admit, but it helps me cope with the fact that raunchy burlesque and vaudeville acts dominated this comedy scene. They were based on crude sexual humor and class limitations. It was almost entirely inappropriate and useless for classrooms. And I haven't even mentioned the overwhelming popularity of comedic minstrel shows.[17]

So let's flash forward to the post–Civil War era, the authors that breathed fresh life into comedic stylings, and the modern tools for classroom retention that developed from their efforts.

Comedy of the Post–Civil War Era

Mark Twain was the first person to become popular using humor in a way that was both accessible to and appropriate for modern students. He also used humor in a way that was, you know, funny. That's not the reason why we are studying him right now. The reason we are studying him is that he was the first popular humorist whose works were unabashedly representative of the emerging American culture. Comedy is about knowing your target audience (see chapter 2). Humor that works to get an SAT-prep class back on track almost definitely won't work to get a loud batch of kindergarteners to clean up the dress-up corner.

You want to see an American quote? Eat a big helping of this:

Travel is fatal to prejudice, bigotry, and narrow-mindedness.[18]

That's a pretty American quote right there. I mean, in Europe, people travel to different countries just for a fun afternoon lark, yet it doesn't usually seem to decrease their intolerance of neighboring cultures (source: like 30 percent of the Europeans in my Facebook feed).

But in America, it's usually an effective burn to reply, "Have you been there?" when someone says something derogatory about one region, such as that all Californians are lazy hippies, or that all New Yorkers are callous, or that all people from Vermont can be tapped for delicious maple syrup.

My point is, being good at zinging a class back into focus requires you to be as much of an anthropologist as you are a comedian. Most engaging modern American teachers need to wear multiple hats, primarily because of climate change but also because truly effective comedy is as much about delivery as it is about researching your target audience. I know what you're saying, "If only there were a chapter in this very book devoted to recognizing and harnessing your target audience. If only it were the very next chapter." To that I say, "Yeah, if only," then I sigh and stare at a nondescript spot on my office wall.

Okay, my points have been established. Irrefutably, I might add, because you have no way to give any input into this book. So let's wrap up the history of comedy and the study of comedy in terms of reading retention, and get on to the instructional portion.

In 2007, S. V. Hellman created "seven steps to success" for using humor in the classroom.[19] I like these, not because they provide a rubric with which you can become a good comedian, but because they provide boundaries so you can avoid using humor to distract a class, look boring, say something inappropriate, get fired, lose your place in heaven, and/or cause grass to wilt and streetlights to turn off when you walk by. Yeah, there's a lot at stake, but that's okay because there are only seven simple steps (and I skipped two of them).

S. V. Hellman's Seven Steps to Comedy Success

1. **Be yourself.**
   My take: Recognizing who you are and how your students perceive you is a key part of constructing a quick, effective joke. You may be surprised to learn that I am a twitchy, nervous, excited teacher because we can all agree my writing style is enchantingly smooth. So making mistakes is a great way to bring a class back around. During a complicated math problem, I'll often make a mistake. This is not just because it is an effective teaching tool, but because I'm actually not that great at math. Someone will inevitably point out my mistake, and I'll say, "Yes! I did that as a teaching tool, and not because I'm actually not that great at math," then mutter loudly to myself, "Yes, I've got them totally fooled." This often causes the class to pay attention, hoping to spot another mistake because

they'll be rewarded with a joke. If you're wondering what type of teaching style you have and what jokes work best for you, check out "The Grand Opening" joke type in chapter 3.

2. **Pick your spots.**
I've said it before and I'll say it again: We're not here to be funny. We're here to teach using the most effective tools possible. Often, hours will pass in between two of my jokes; if I see my class is alert and listening, there's no need. "If it ain't broke, don't make a joke" is a great platitude for effective comedy use in the classroom.

3. **Be politically correct.**
Teachers don't want to hurt their students' feelings, but we often do so unintentionally. If you're worried that you might be going too "blue" for your class (or if you're not worried but you should be), chapter 4 goes in depth about many common traps teachers often fall for.

4. **Know your audience.**
To figure out what type of humor an audience will enjoy, you need to know their ages, maturity levels, backgrounds, etc. It's kind of like reading an actuarial table: The type of comedy most likely to get a good response depends on certain demographics. Younger people tend to like more random humor. Adult students often prefer situational comedy. Some people don't respond to any type of humor at all (such as the people who make actuarial tables). I will cover the optimal audience for each style of joke over the next few chapters.

7. **Acknowledge others' humor.**
Yeah, I know I skipped #5 and #6. I'm not sitting on a pirate's shoulder, so why do you expect me to parrot everything?

One of the weirdest, most confusing experiences I had as a student came in my senior year of high school. My economics class was taught by a zany, beloved older gentleman. A few of my friends were in the class, it was exciting, and I was having a good time. Then one day, the school counselor called me in. He said the teacher had said I was extremely disruptive and was considering kicking me out of the class. I had never been told this before, and keep in mind I *was* a pretty disruptive student in all my classes, so I took it seriously. For the next two weeks, I said literally not one word unless called upon for an answer. Not one word. My friends asked me if everything was okay with my family and life—my silent behavior was so out of line for my usual self. After those two weeks, the teacher told the counselor that my behavior had gotten even more disruptive and he was removing me from his class. This caused real trouble for me, as I needed the class to graduate, so I had to rearrange my entire school schedule around the other economics class.

I was baffled about the situation until some older friends of mine came back into town from college. "Oh yeah," they said. "He kicks out anyone that's funnier than him." Three weeks later, it was discovered that he had given out answers to a state examination "to be funny," and he was fired despite being only one year from retirement. So let that be a lesson to you: acknowledge others' humor. That's the lesson right? Because that's the lesson 17-year-old me learned.

Just kidding. The real lesson 17-year-old me learned is that comedy is a weapon. It can provide relief to those in the deepest stages of grief, it can enrage the low-self-esteem comedians, it can kill.

It *can* kill.

It killed Socrates.

 That's called a "call back": for some reason, referring back to something you mentioned like 20 minutes ago makes people laugh, even though it's not actually a joke.

So Aristophanes wrote a satirical play called *Clouds*, which portrays Socrates as a morality-rejecting rabble-rouser who spends most of his time inciting dissent against the government.

Twenty-four years later, Socrates was tried and executed for corrupting youth. Did Aristophanes's play influence popular opinion of Socrates? Did it cement Socrates as a bad guy in the eyes of the people? Could likely be true. Might not be, but we don't have time for counterpoints right now. On to the workbook!

CHAPTER 2
JOKEMAKING TECHNIQUES WORKBOOK

Reading Your Target Audience

So a guy goes in to meet with a divorce attorney. "I have the funniest joke," says the lawyer. "You are going to lose everything!" The guy says, "That's not funny." The attorney says, "That's weird, your ex-wife found it hilarious!"

—Some comedic genius (just kidding, it's only me)

Before you can even do step one of using humor to successfully increase retention, you have to get to know your audience. Actually, I guess that counts as a step. Let me try again:

Before you can even do step two of using humor to successfully increase retention, you have do step one. Step one is to get to know your audience.

Although there are certain universal constants that link all audiences, the hard fact is that most jokes that work for one target audience probably won't work for another. The quip that was a hit at the break-room watercooler almost definitely won't work for your emerging economics middle-school course. The main reason for this is...well, the main reason for this is that the joke probably has nothing to do with emerging economics. But the second-most main reason is that the things that make middle schoolers laugh rarely overlaps with the things that elicit laughter from break-room teachers clutching cups of water with nicotine-stained fingers.

One of my favorite classroom exercises involves teaching the statistical concepts of mean, median, and mode. When I was a student, way back when the Big Bang was just a weather forecast, I never understood why there was a concept of median or mode. I assumed that statisticians liked to make up weird ways to look at data and give them stupid names that I was supposed to memorize. So I walked the taut rope between "learning what median and mode were enough to pass my tests" and "not learning them enough where I would ever remember them again after the tests, thus freeing up valuable brain power for remembering the lyrics to hip-hop jams."

It turns out median and mode are critical concepts in evaluating whether or not someone is using statistics to lie to you, most likely during election season. So when my classes with college-bound teens or grad school–bound business majors touch on the subject, I make sure to hammer it home with a fun anecdote that is rife with opportunity for humor:

I tell the class, "Imagine you all live in a coal-mining town." I then pick one of the nicest, most social students in the class—let's call him Cujo. I'll say, "Cujo here owns the coal-mining plant, and you all work for him. He pays each of you $20,000 a year. He makes $1 billion a year." Naturally, this can elicit some good-natured ribbing from the class toward Cujo's tight-fisted monetary policies, but I try not to participate since, you know, I was the one who made him a coal-mine owner in the first place so to make fun of him for it is super passive-aggressive.

I'll then say, "Let's say a reporter wants to write about the typical family in town. They come in and find out the average salary is millions and millions of dollars. Does that mean the typical family in town is super rich? Of course not—everyone in town but one person is borderline impoverished. So statisticians needed to come up with other ways to assess what's 'typical.' One of those ways is mode: What's the most common salary in town? $20,000. Much more reflective of the normal income. Another is median. What's the middle salary in town? $20,000. Both of those paint a much better picture of what the typical town household is like."

It's a simple and fun way to express median and mode, and one that leads to comedic opportunities...for the right audience. For the wrong audience, it is a big, elaborate waste of time. A class of eight-year-olds won't understand most of the real-world concepts involved (unless it's a class of eight-year-olds in 1895, who will understand it because most of them probably just got done with their shifts at a local coal mine).

On average, each individual in this picture is holding $10,000 (if you include the ATM machine).

Once I substitute-taught an SAT-prep class for an extremely affluent private Catholic girls' high school, set in the lofty hills of Southern California. When I saw that the lesson included mean, median, and mode, I quickly launched into the example. It was less than effective, and it was only after minutes of trying to get their minds around what a "typical" town household was that I realized my problem: to these students, the billionaire coal-mine owner was the typical household. I mistakenly assumed that everyone can just look at a town with one rich person and a bunch of poor people and conclude, "Wow, life for the typical family here is pretty bad." I was wrong.

Side note: What the class of Catholic–high-school girls did find engaging was the stain on the back of my pants, which was caused by me having sat on my son's chocolate ice cream spoon right before class. Sadly, I was not able to spin that into a positive teaching moment, as I was not aware the stain even existed until I had reached the end of the three-hour class. What is the point of this anecdote, you might ask? I don't know, I'm just hoping it has some use because otherwise I endured hours of extreme humiliation for absolutely no reason.

Misreading your target audience is more common than you might think, and it happens even at the highest levels of comedy. It also occurs at my level of comedy.

Now, there's a trick to not misreading your target audience that works far better for teaching than it does for comedy writing or stand-up: don't make up your jokes ahead of time.

This chapter has a bunch of formulae for making up quick jokes in the heat of the moment. Even if you are horrible at improvisation, it's okay. I'm horrible at improvisation—writing the average quip for this book takes me five minutes of staring at the wall with my jaw hanging open. But I can make a quick joke that gets a class engaged because I've studied the templates covered in this chapter and I know the specifics for what makes each subset of students laugh.

So, let's begin!

Don't casinos pump in oxygen to keep people awake? Schools should do that. Except with aerosolized coffee.

It was a rainy Seattle Sunday, the patter of the drops on the classroom windows were as repetitive as the term "rainy Seattle Sunday." Instead of curling up in bed with a good book, or whatever millennials are doing these days (probably curling up in bed with a bad book because all media made after [your birth year plus 25] sucks), several teens had to drag themselves into my SAT test-prep class for three hours of super-fun math review.

When the clock struck "begin class o'clock," I surveyed a troublesome scene: more hanging heads than a gallows, droopy eyelids, and students hadn't even pulled out their books (not even to use as pillows). Outside, the steady gray drizzle compounded the sleepy scene with gentle, endless white noise. There was no way these students were going to retain a three-hour lesson, not in their current state of mental blurriness.

This was definitely a cold crowd. A cold crowd lacks energy; a warm crowd is alert but distracted. I needed a spark, so I quickly surveyed the room.

"Hector, your shirt is red," I said to one student I knew was particularly into fashion. "Is red your favorite color to wear?"

"Dunno," Hector grumbled. I might need more than a spark to get things started; this situation might call for full-blown arson. Not necessarily a bad thing: arson can be fun, as long as it is carefully controlled.

"What's your least favorite color to wear?" I continued.

"Dunno," he repeated.

"Dunno," I echoed. "But I know what you do know—coordinate geometry! Come on up and demonstrate a problem…OR tell me a color you hate to wear."

Now Hector was motivated to contribute, "I guess I hate wearing yellow."

Perfect, I had my setup. Now I just needed my punch line. I glanced around the room for someone wearing yellow and spotted Shannon. Bubbly, blonde, and self-assured, yellow-shirted Shannon would be the perfect unwitting target for some lighthearted fun.

"Whoa," I exclaimed, pointing at her. "Shots fired directly at Shannon."

This garnered some chuckles but, more importantly, it ratcheted up the tension. Hector immediately started to walk back his yellow comment, and the whole class tuned in to watch. The class had flipped from borderline comatose to passionately engaged with the power of one joke. One extremely formulaic joke that can be learned by any teacher.

My well-placed quip wasn't due to an innate ability to improv jokes. Heck, as I write it, half of this chapter currently says, "[Evan, put a joke here next time you have a few hours to think of one.]" I was simply taking a time-tested joke-writing formula and filling in the blanks. My challenge was not to create the perfect joke to wake everyone up, but simply to read the room and determine which formula would best fit the situation.

The only remaining ingredient missing was timing. This is why I love teaching humor to teachers more than to anyone else: teachers have naturally developed their own speaking rhythms, so they automatically have a consistent patter. It doesn't matter if you've botched the punch line to every joke you've ever told. Just say these simple formulae in your usual cadence, and you will get results.

That's what this chapter is about: classic joke-writing structures that leave little room for whiffs. Let's examine the one outlined in the above anecdote.

Formula 1: Schlemiel-Schlimazel
Age Group: Tweens and Teens
Cold/Warm Audience: Cold

There's an old Yiddish explanation: the schlemiel is the person who trips and spills his soup; the schlimazel is the person the soup gets spilled upon. The ultimate goal is getting a student to say something that seems innocuous, then twisting it to sound like a slight against another student.

Without being mean or creating a hostile class environment, of course.

Obviously, the key to this is that the schlemiel has to be totally innocent. We're not trying to hurt anyone's feelings here. The easy key to that is to elicit a very general statement of preference: least favorite color, choice of bookbag versus backpack, choice of school supplies (pencil versus pen, etc.). If you know your class better, you could elicit their least favorite sport (then pick a schlimazel you know plays that sport) or least favorite subject (it's great if they pick the subject you are teaching because then you get to be the schlimazel—nothing like rebellion against a teacher for getting other students to pay attention). Those are very vague things that the schlimazel will never take personally and never get upset about.

Bad topics are ones that lead the schlemiel directly into saying something disparaging about a group of people: least favorite form of espionage, etc.

Just kidding about that espionage thing. Although, just in case you are suspicious one of your students is a spy, I recommend you take a step back and read the book, *Let's All Mellow Out and Stop Thinking Everyone Is a Spy* by Joseph McCarthy.

Restaurant secret: a good waiter will always memorize regular customers' favorite orders by spilling the food into their laps.

ACTIVITY I

For each prompt, identify:
- if there is a schlemiel and a schlimazel
- if so, who they are
- what the "soup" is that is being spilled
- whether this is an appropriate joke to make

Prompt 1

Karen and Jan both have green backpacks.

Teacher: Wow Jan, how do you feel about Karen copying your stylish choice of green backpack?

ANSWER

Schlemiel: None. Jan is not "spilling soup" on Karen, and, in fact, Jan's style has been complimented.

Schlimazel: Karen. She is being portrayed as a fashion copycat.

Soup: Bad fashion choice.

Appropriate: Almost. Backpack color isn't something students put a lot of thought or expressiveness into, which makes it a good subject. However, a better joke would have a schlemiel to ratchet up the tension.

Prompt 2

Karen and Jan both have green backpacks.

Teacher: Wow, Karen and Jan both have green backpacks. But Mo's backpack is black...I guess you didn't feel like cc'ing Mo on the green backpack email? Cold-blooded.

ANSWER

Schlemiel: Karen and Jan. They are being painted as actively ignoring Mo.

Schlimazel: Mo. He is being portrayed as being left out.

Soup: The coordination email, the cause of Mo's manufactured distress.

Appropriate: Yes. This is farcical enough that no student should misinterpret it and think there's actually a green backpack conspiracy. If a student does misinterpret the situation, however, it can be safely defused and steered toward the teacher: "I'm just kidding, of course. There's no green backpack email going around. Or, if there is, I certainly got left out. What the heck, Karen and Jan?"

Prompt 3

Karen and Jan both have messy hair.

Teacher: Wow, Karen and Jan both have messy hair. Mo, your hair looks great, you should give them tips.

ANSWER

Schlemiel: None.

Schlimazel: Karen and Jan are on the receiving end of the ridicule.

Soup: Bad hair.

Appropriate: No. Don't make fun of a student's appearance. As a general rule, jokes that involve a student's looks, specific fashion choices, or grooming/hygiene are never a good idea.

Prompt 4

Karen has a hairband, Jan does not.

Teacher: Karen, how's the hairband treating you? Jan, you don't have a hairband? So you're making a statement to Karen that you don't like her hairband?

ANSWER

Schlemiel: Jan. She's being portrayed as spilling hairband hatred onto Karen.

Schlimazel: Karen. She's receiving the hairband-fashion questioning.

Soup: Choice of hair accessory.

Appropriate: Sure. As long as we don't say something qualifying about the hairband, like the quality of its appearance or how expensive it looks, this joke is innocuous. Keep it as arbitrary as possible: whether or not to wear a hairband is not something the average student puts a lot of time and energy into.

Prompt 5

Karen has a necklace, Jan does not.

Teacher: Karen, how's the necklace treating you? Jan, you don't have a necklace? So you're making a statement to Karen that you don't like her necklace?

ANSWER

Schlemiel: Jan. She's being portrayed as spilling necklace hatred onto Karen.

Schlimazel: Karen. She's receiving the necklace-fashion questioning.

Soup: Choice of neck/chest accessory.

Appropriate: No. Never call attention to the area around a teenage girl's chest. The last thing a student needs is for everyone in the class to stare at her "necklace."

Prompt 6

Karen and Jan both have heavy coats on.

Teacher: Wow, Karen and Jan, you both have heavy coats on. That's what homeless people wear. Are you sleeping in the streets? Can I help?

ANSWER

Schlemiel: The teacher. The teacher is making the ridiculous assumption that big coats equals homeless.

Schlimazel: Karen and Jan.

Soup: Coats resembling those worn by homeless people.

Appropriate: Never. The teacher should never be the schlemiel. Even with more mundane jokes, teachers have such authority that it magnifies any perceived slight, no matter how small or how sarcastically delivered (or how little the class thinks of us).

Prompt 7

Karen and Jan both have heavy coats on.

Teacher: Hey, Karen and Jan both have heavy coats on. I don't have a heavy coat on today. You must know something I don't. That happens to me a lot and it's depressing.

ANSWER

Schlemiel: Karen and Jan. They are wearing coats to illustrate how ill prepared the teacher is.

Schlimazel: The teacher.

Soup: A lack of being informed.

Appropriate: Sort of. It's okay for teachers to be schlimazels, but it can undermine our image as knowledge experts. Only make teachers schlimazels if we can "pull up" into our skill sets. "Hey, Karen and Jan both have heavy coats on. I don't have a heavy coat on today. You must know something I don't. That happens to me a lot and it's depressing. But I know something you don't, and that's the four acceptable ways to break up two independent clauses. Turn to page 27 in your grammar workbooks."

Now that we've outlined the ways to tell a schlemiel from a schlimazel (and also how to identify the inappropriate execution of this formula), let's learn to write.

The first step ties in with knowing your target audience. There's not always a need for this joke; sometimes the class is alert and a teacher getting humorous just delays the learning. Plus the more you do it, the more they will see it coming. Chapter 4 will go into detail about the destruction a telegraphed punch line can have on class focus. I recommend using the schlemiel-schlimazel only once every five classes max.

You'll probably find you need it even less frequently, as its goal is to shake up a normally attentive class during "weird days." Those may include:

- particularly bleak, sleepy weather
- an unexpectedly brain-taxing event—for instance, if the class happens right after an AP examination
- the first class of the morning after a lengthy school break

Knowing if your class will be a good target audience for this setup requires both anticipating when you might have a problem class and reading the room to confirm that, yes, everyone here is a bit slower in terms of enthusiasm and mental "juice."

ACTIVITY II

Identify if each situation is a good fit for a schlemiel-schlimazel joke, based on the three criteria listed on the previous page:

A. Scene: A morning class after winter break
    Crowd: Lots of yawns, several latecomers, no before-class conversations

B. Scene: A postlunch class after a schoolyard fight
    Crowd: Distracted students buzzing about the brouhaha

C. Scene: The last class on a Friday before the homecoming football game
    Crowd: Lots of school colors being worn, students looking at the clock a lot

D. Scene: A class missing its regular teacher, during a gentle snowstorm
    Crowd: Lots of eyes staring out the window

E. Scene: A rainy day
    Crowd: Elementary-school students who just spent the lunch period inside playing challenging board games

ANSWERS

A. Students' minds take a while to get back into the swing of school after winter break. The class seems as cold as a cow that makes ice cream. A good time for the schlemiel-schlimazel.

B. After watching a schoolyard fight, students will be excited and not sleepy or slowed down. Try a forced transition (discussed later in this chapter). Not a good fit for the schlemiel-schlimazel.

C. The class before the homecoming football game isn't cold or sleepy; they're just distracted. Not a good time for the schlemiel-schlimazel.

D. The class missing its regular teacher is ripe for an engaging back-and-forth, but a substitute teacher isn't the right one for this. They aren't familiar, and even if the gambit works, it might amp the class up to a level that is hard for a temporary teacher to reign in. Plus, a substitute usually can't tell who makes a good candidate for each role in this joke.

E. An elementary-school class that is more mentally taxed than usual and a gray day are two classic ingredients for a schlemiel-schlimazel execution.

Review Problems

QUESTION 1

It's a sleepy morning class. All of these students have at least one characteristic that would make them a good schlimazel except:

A. DeShaun: Hair in an afro, tweed jacket with elbow patches, sunglasses on (indoors), purple pen

B. Delaun: Hair in a messy ponytail, Star of David necklace, oversized gray sweatshirt, topaz ring

C. Marlon: Gold nose stud, "I love opera" T-shirt, greasy black hair, motorcycle gloves

D. Carson: Messy hair, acne scars on chin, hearing aid, prosthetic leg

E. Janelle: Green mohawk, tuxedo T-shirt, spiked wristband, extremely rigid posture

QUESTION 2

You've decided to make Delaun the schlemiel and Janelle the schlimazel. Based on the characteristics from question 1, what would be the best joke to make?

A. "How long did it take you to do your hair, Delaun? You're making a statement that Janelle spends too much time on her looks!"

B. "If a necklace-fearing monster attacks, Delaun's necklace will protect her, and the monster will then attack Janelle. Janelle's only hope is that the monster is looking for a menu and thinks Janelle is a waiter!"

C. "Delaun's sweatshirt is a direct attack on Janelle. She's saying Janelle is a posture show-off. You can't even see how much Delaun is slouching in that sweatshirt."

D. "Janelle has a spiked bracelet, Delaun has a spiky ring. I'd take Delaun in a competition to see who can accidentally injure themselves first."

E. "Comfy sweatshirt, Delaun. Did you wear it to make Janelle feel overdressed?"

ANSWERS

1. D. Messy hair is a matter of hygiene, don't go there. Acne scars can be a source of low self-esteem. Calling attention to the hearing aid and prosthetic leg calls attention to a disability. Leave him alone.

2. E. Don't call attention to sloppy hygiene, which eliminates A. Steer away from religious references, like B. C spills soup on both Delaun and Janelle. Similarly, D takes equal shots at both ladies.

Formula 2: The Forced Transition
Target Audience: Teens and Adults
Cold/Warm Audience: Warm

I was not sure what Janine's deal was, but she had been acting quite bizarre. The GRE test-prep student had come to class an hour late the first night. She did not bring her book, and her phone rang twice soon after she sat down. Fifteen minutes later, she asked to use the restroom, gathered her belongings, and left. She did not return.

The next time the class met, a few days later, Janine was absent. The students rightfully complained that she had been a little distracting.

Michelle, the resident wit, quipped, "Is she still in the bathroom? Should someone go check?" She then pondered, "Maybe she has a secret boyfriend her parents won't let her date, and she's using the class as an excuse to meet him."

While I found this debate fascinating, I had to cut it short ASAP. Nothing good can come from ostracizing a student. It would hamper the dynamic of the group activities I had planned (if Janine showed up), and it certainly wouldn't lead to higher test scores.

But Michelle was holding court—to sternly correct or hush her meant risking losing the class's favor. So I lowered my voice to a pregnant whisper:

"You know who else might have a secret boyfriend?"

The class was at full attention, expecting a juicy secret. I continued:

"Roald Amundsen. Was his secret boyfriend Robert Scott? Is that why they were racing each other to the South Pole in 1911, because it was the only place they wouldn't be persecuted for their love? Let's turn to page 317 of our reading comprehension primers and find out."

First, take note that this is for a warmed-up audience. Michelle had already cracked a few jokes to get the class chuckling, so all I needed was to direct their attention away from her and onto the first part of the lesson. In fact, your audience will always be warm, since they are interested in whatever current topic the jokester is riffing on. You just have to transfer their attention to the new topic without them cooling off too much, just like transferring a tray of freshly baked cookies onto wax paper before they cool off (proper cookie making is important to me).

The humor of this relies upon the subject matter having little or nothing to do with the topic that is being transitioned away from. If I had said, "You know who else might have a secret boyfriend? Queen Victoria, who had lots of affairs. Turn to page 232 to read about her in a reading comprehension passage," it would have been a fine transition, but not a forced one. To be clear, that's great. If it somehow happens that the topic is related to whatever is next on the lesson plan, wonderful, just get there. But that will almost never happen. The topics will usually be totally unrelated, which is why we focus on spotlighting the stark difference with humor.

The specific formula is elegant in its simplicity: Simply state, "Do you know who/what else was [whatever the topic is]?" Then state the next part of your lesson plan.

Really, the only way to botch this joke is to drag out the timing. As with all jokes in the classroom, the goal is not to get a laugh or entertain the audience; the goal is to increase retention and attention. The class is discussing an exciting topic, and we want to steer them to one they won't like as much without making things feel like too much of a comedown.

The rhythm shakes out like this:

Teacher: Do you know who else may have a secret boyfriend? [beat*]

Roald Amundsen. Maybe his race against Scott to the South Pole was so they could have a relationship. Let's turn to page 245 and find out.

Note how the punch line is fluid and that there is no pause between "relationship" and "Let's turn to page 245." A pause there would bring down the excitement, and we're trying to carry over the class's excitement for the previous topic to the next one. By using the unexpected transition as a metaphorical stepladder, there isn't as much disappointment in the drop in levity between the two subjects.

ACTIVITY

Write a forced transition joke to link the following prompts:

Prompt 1

You need to talk about the history behind the Gilded Age, but the class has been discussing the latest episode of "Let's Talk about a Gory Murder."

---

* In scriptwriting, a *beat* is defined as "a pause long enough to let the magnitude of your statement sink in, but not too long so as to mess up the timing of the joke." The length of the beat is fluid and depends on how the tempo is flowing: If the class/teacher is speaking quickly and sharing lots of ideas rapidly, the beat doesn't need to be longer than a second or two. For more slow-moving patter, a longer beat is usually right. Teachers tend to have a natural ability to recognize the current tempo, so "whatever length feels right" usually works. We just have to avoid pausing so long that our students figure out a punch line is coming. Punch lines should always be sneaky. Nothing turns an audience off more than the realization that they are expected to laugh. Plus, telegraphing a punch line increases the penalty for failure; a quickly slipped-in joke that doesn't elicit laughter is just entertaining patter, but a drawn-out setup with a pause before the punch line and a pause for laughter can lead to a black void of silence that sucks the soul out of the room.

ANSWER

"You know who loved to talk about gory murder? People from the Gilded Age, let's learn about their history."

NOTE: Always take a look to see if there's a natural transition, even if it means sacrificing the joke. Jokes are like soldiers, you must be willing to sacrifice any of them if it means winning the war against disinterested pupils. Here, you might have come up with, "You know what follows gory murder? Well, in the case of the gory killings of the Civil War, it was followed by what's known as the Gilded Age." The joke falls away, but it's fine because the class is interested in the aftermath of bloodshed.

Prompt 2

Your lesson plan calls for opening with an explanation of the Pythagorean theorem, but your high-school class is abuzz over a fight that happened in the halls earlier.

ANSWER

"You know what always helps me win a fight? The Pythagorean theorem. It also helps me figure out the lengths of the sides of a right triangle..."

Prompt 3

A lesson on rain forest precipitation derails into a discussion about the president's environmental policies.

ANSWER

"I only have three words to say about our president: rain forest precipitation. In 1985, it averaged five inches during the wet season..."

Naturally, your answers will be different. Rather than focusing on the details when analyzing these answers, focus on whether you managed to mirror the structure.

Formula 3: The 1-2-3
Target Audience: 3- to 12-Year-Olds
Cold/Warm Audience: Cold

I had thought that volunteering to teach music to my 4-year-old twins' class would be simple: I have ample teaching experience, their usual instructors had trained the kids to sit quietly and pay attention, and I like ear pain. However, a rare Southern California thunderstorm had caused the kids to miss their midday playground exercise time. I was now facing the daunting task of trying to teach a dozen squirmy, whispering preschoolers.

"Class, do you know what rhythm is? It's when you do things evenly, like one...two...three...four..." I played a simple tune on my keyboard. Before I could engage them, I needed their attention, and melody is the undisputed champion of catching the attention of small children.

"Rhythm is useful for three reasons. First, it makes the song easy to follow. Second, an easy-to-follow song is simple to dance to. And third, dancing is the best way TO REPEL ZOMBIES." Soon, I had half the class excitedly dancing, attempting to maintain rhythm, while the other half pretended to be zombies who had to stop every time the "humans" were dancing to the music.

All of these children are in danger of being eaten by zombies.

It should come as no surprise that the brains of kids ages 3 to 12 are developing at a fast rate. As such, a 1-2-3 is a simple, repeatable tool to elicit laughter and focus through circumventing the traditional pattern recognition these children have come to expect. It's so simple that this is often the first joke structure that comedians are taught. The formula is as follows:

- Incorporate a list into whatever you are talking about. "Today, our studies will cover the three reasons World War II broke out," "There are three tips to remember when doing fractions," etc.

The first two items are normal, the third takes it in a new direction: either something outlandishly unrelated or an unexpected item that relates to the list.

Outlandishly unrelated:

- "Today our studies will include algebra, cursive, and fighting alligators. Yeah, the first two don't sound so bad, now do they?"

Unexpectedly related item:

- "There are three tips to remember when doing fractions: find a least common multiple when adding or subtracting fractions, divide fractions by flipping one fraction upside down then multiplying, and stifle your screams into your fist so no one around you realizes how much you hate fractions."

ACTIVITY I

Come up with a list of three *normal* things to fill out each prompt. Naturally, we will explore how to change the third item into one that provides humor (and, more importantly, elicits focus). But let's begin by just getting used to previewing topics in lists of three:

Prompt 1
There were three main reasons for the Civil War...

Prompt 2
There are three reasons you should learn the formula for percent change...

Prompt 3
All the letters in the alphabet can be divided into three categories...

Prompt 4
Class, if you don't stop talking, you won't learn about...

Prompt 5
There are three rules for our field trip...

ANSWERS

(These are just suggestions; if you came up with a different set of lists, you should still feel confident that you have the foundation it takes to master this joke strategy.)

1. There were three main reasons for the Civil War: a dispute over political control between states and the federal government, differing views on slavery, and territorial expansion disagreements.

2. There are three reasons you should learn the formula for percent change: we use it all the time in real life, it helps you figure out how much money you are making on an investment, and it's an efficient way to solve a lot of word problems involving stocks and reselling purchased goods.

3. All the letters in the alphabet can be divided into three categories: consonants, vowels, and the letter Y.

4. Class, if you don't stop talking, you won't learn about math you need to know to survive in the real world, history mistakes you need to not repeat, and my test-grading policy.

5. There are three rules for our field trip: stick with your buddy, don't wander off, and use the bathroom before getting on the bus.

Now that we've got our foundations for writing, let's work on delivery. It's imperative that you do this practice before moving on to writing punch lines. It will ensure you know how to recognize a tightly delivered joke. You want them to flow naturally. When the student's mind notices a well-delivered joke, that student will naturally pay more attention to see if there are any other interesting jokes hiding within your patter. Blam! Maximal engagement is achieved.

NOTE: We're not doing 1-2-3s so the students will memorize the list of three right away. That would be pointless, as one-third of that list is just a punch line. We do 1-2-3s so distracted students will notice our entertaining jokes and pay more attention, increasing retention for future lists of facts.

First, however, we've got to rehearse to fully understand our own natural rhythm.

ACTIVITY II

Required:

- Answers from Activity I
- Device capable of recording video and audio

1. Posture yourself how you normally do in the classroom. If you stand, then stand. If you normally sit, then sit. If you normally do something other than stand or sit, then you're doing something wrong.

2. Start recording.

3. Take your five lists from Activity I and read them aloud. Don't overthink your delivery. There's a good chance you naturally have the right rhythm and cadence to deliver a 1-2-3.

Now, play back your recording and analyze your speech pattern. Look for the following issues:

- Change in tone. You want to be delivering all three items in the same way. Changing tone, volume, or speed on the third item can telegraph a punch line or otherwise encourage your audience to tune you out.

- Monotone. Even though this was read and not improvised, you want to make sure that your vocal inflections are normal for a human from Earth (oh, how you've got them all fooled!). A robotic delivery runs the risk that no one will even listen to the second item in your list, much less the payoff third item.

- Facial expressions. Another way to turn off an audience is delivering the punch line with a smile, eyelid lift, or sassy head sway. I knew a teacher once who was quite funny, but she was puzzled as to why her students (sixth graders) never laughed at her jokes. I asked her to make a recording of her teaching. Before each punch line, she would pause, inhale, crack a huge smile, then deliver the payoff with a vaudeville-esque lilt in her voice. At times, there were audible groans before she even delivered the punch lines. Students don't like to know the punch line is coming, and they especially don't like the implication that they are expected to laugh.

If you notice any of the above issues, record yourself again running through all five lists. Before moving on to actual punch-line development, you want to nail the surprisingly difficult matter of Reading Three-Part Lists Like a Normal Person. So don't proceed until you can get at least one good recording of all five lists without displaying any of the issues listed above.

The whole purpose for this focus on making sure you deliver lists evenly involves attention. If a student hears three list items, then realizes, "Hey, wait a minute...one of those list items was funny," it will make them pay more attention to future statements—no matter how rote or pattern based they may seem. Score! We've got lean-forward attention in the classroom.

But before we can get there, we must make sure our punch line has some punch...er, some kick to it. There are some rules to this because what would free-flowing comedy be without *a rigid set of requirements*:

- The third item in your list must be an exaggeration. It can't just take the list in a new direction; it must be an item that can stand on its own as a larger-than-life statement.

- The third item needs to be immediately recognizable as farce. Three- to 12-year-olds aren't the fine-tuned sarcasm detectors we embittered adults are. That means we need to create a third item with zero relation to the list topic. Your target audience will easily spot the ridiculousness of "There are three types of letters: consonants, vowels, and killer bears." But it could easily miss the joke if delivered as, "There are three types of letters: consonants, vowels, and killer consonants."

Got it? I don't believe you. Prove it to me with...

ACTIVITY III

Materials:
- Device capable of recording video and audio (hopefully you didn't throw it away after the last activity)
- Answer lists from Activity II

1. Go over each of the five lists from Activity II, removing the third item and replacing it with a punch line. Make sure to heed the requirements outlined for an effective 1-2-3 payoff.

2. Now line up the meter. You want the first two items to be similar in length and structure. They don't have to be boilerplate copies of each other, but they should take about the same time to deliver. That's how we quickly establish a pattern.

3. Adjust your punch line so it either fits the length established by the first two items or is much shorter.

RIGHT
"There are three great reasons to learn the formula for percent change: we use it all the time in real life, it tells you how much money is made on an investment, and bees use it to attract a mate."

RIGHT
"There are three great reasons to learn the formula for percent change: we use it all the time in real life, it tells you how much money is made on an investment, and it tastes great!"

WRONG
"There are three great reasons to learn the formula for percent change: we use it all the time in real life, it tells you how much money is made on an investment, and our country was founded upon the Bill of Rights, which starts with 'Thou shalt allow citizens to calculate percent change.'"

TEACHER'S NOTE: It's not unusual for a teacher to become uneasy with modifying a list of three down to two items. After all, there's something to be said for a complete preview of all three items in a lesson. If this is making you nervous, you can always correct yourself, either immediately after reading the list or when you come to the third item in your actual lesson plan. "There are three types of letters: consonants, vowels, and killer bears. And, by killer bears, I mean 'the letter Y.'" Alternatively, when you come to the letter Y in your lesson, say, "There is a *third* type of letter, and no, it's not killer bears. It's the letter Y, which has its own category."

Now that you've written five solid 1-2-3 jokes, it's time to rehearse!

ACTIVITY IV, Part 1

Materials:
- Device capable of recording audio and video (now you know why they sell smartphones in packs of three!)
- List of jokes from Activity III

1. Again, stand/sit as you would when normally teaching a class.
2. Record yourself telling each of the 1-2-3 jokes.
3. Watch yourself, again trying to spot common issues.

This is where we bring it all together, so it's expected that common mistakes will creep back in. That's okay, my aunt used to have a saying: "A comedian who records themselves and recognizes areas that need improvement is better than anything your Uncle Steve has ever done."

Again, keep practicing until you can rattle off all five lists in one session with no change in cadence. Congratulations, you're ready for a live audience!

ACTIVITY IV, Part 2

Materials:
- Your list of five 1-2-3 jokes from Activity IV
- A funny friend or colleague or someone too polite to walk away

1. Find the funniest person you know.
2. Ask for feedback, then recite your jokes. If you can't meet them in person, it's acceptable to send them your footage, but there's something extra that comes with rehearsing live.

NOTE: Here, your funny friend might suggest something that may seem to run contrary to the principles outlined here. *That's okay.* Sometimes a bit of divergence is just what a 1-2-3 joke needs to raise its chance to "land" (engage an audience). In fact, if your friend (or you) thinks a joke is lacking punch but can't quite vocalize exactly what it needs, try incorporating one (and only one) of these common tools:

The IDK Stutter Step

Before the third list item, pause for a very quick beat, then add, "I don't know" before immediately delivering the punch line. "There are three types of letters: consonants, vowels, and, I don't know, ice cream sandwiches." The key is to understate the "I don't know," foreshadowing that there might be a punch line coming up without full-on telegraphing it. This is an especially useful step for educators who are having trouble with their delivery sounding wooden or too scripted.

Excitement for Pain

If the third statement is something averse, it can often be punched up by delivering it with over-the-top enthusiasm. "Class, if you don't stop talking, you won't learn about math you need to know to survive in the real world, history mistakes you need to not repeat, and [smile] how great it feels to get yelled at by ME!" This is especially great for teachers who are having trouble not telegraphing their punch lines: it's okay to telegraph it if you do it in a facetious way.

The Speedy Getaway

This is an all-purpose tool that works with almost any joke formula, but especially with the 1-2-3. As soon as you finish saying the third-item punch line, immediately go into your lesson plan. Your goal should be to almost sound like you are interrupting yourself (to be clear, interrupting yourself is rude: raise your hand first, and wait for you to call on yourself). "There were three main reasons for the Civil War: a dispute over political control between states and the federal government, different views on slavery, and Instagram drama—turn your books to page 183." This tool can be particularly useful for engaging a class of budding tweens that are "too cool" to enjoy jokes: by showing that you don't even care whether they laugh or not, it makes you seem more aloof and relatable.

TEACHER'S NOTE: If a joke is landing, don't try to add effect with these tools. The goal is simply to give an engaging transition into a lesson plan, not write the world's best joke.

Well done! You've developed jokes from scratch and tested them out on a knowledgeable audience. Take their feedback, incorporate it, and run it back for them to see if they approve.

REVIEW QUESTIONS: 1-2-3

1. Which of these lists best completes the 1-2-3 joke as applied to a lesson plan about vegetables for third graders?

A fruit is a seed-bearing part of a plant that develops from an ovary, whereas vegetables are all other parts, including _____

A. roots, leaves, and bizarro leaves.
B. roots, leaves, and the underground chamber of death.
C. roots, goots, and zoots.
D. roots, leaves, and...giant eyeballs?
E. roots, leaves, and, I don't know, stems.

2. Your 1-2-3 joke, "There are three rules of probability: the multiplication rule, the addition rule, and giant toothbrushes," isn't landing with your funny friend. Which of the following illustrates the best way to change the punch line?

A. and, I don't know, toothbrushes
B. and the casino-always-wins rule
C. and the rule that too many toothbrushes will drive math students insane
D. and the contents of a school toilet rule
E. and tiny toothbrushes

3. Match the "feedback from your funny friend" to the tool that will address it:

A. "Your delivery sounds like a robot met a metronome and had a baby."
B. "Your jokes are good, but I saw some graffiti saying you are the most boring teacher."
C. "You smile during the third item and it ruins the delivery."

   1. IDK stutter-step
   2. Excitement for pain
   3. Speedy getaway

ANSWERS

1. When you have two one-word items in a 1-2-3, you want the third item to be just as short. That eliminates B. Answer choice A has a third item far too similar to an earlier item, running the risk that a student will misinterpret it as actual fact (it really happens). C has a zany

second item rather than a normal one. While E correctly uses the IDK stutter-step, the third item is fact, not farce. That leaves D, the third item. D is short and something that even a young child knows would be silly as part of a plant. In addition, expressing the third item as a question wakes students up. It's easy for students to tune out even the most ridiculous statements, but phrasing it as a question allows for a pause so they can think about it and say, "Wait a minute…"

2. Here there are two issues: One, toothbrushes, in themselves, are not silly enough to complete a 1-2-3 setup. Two, there could be much more parallel between the structure of the first two items and the punch line. A and C don't address either rule. E changes the punch line, but making things smaller does not make them funnier. Sometimes making things bigger makes them funnier, though. D is lowbrow humor, which can cause loss of focus as young students focus on whether they can now use toilet humor. That leaves B: adding a "rule" parallels "the division rule, the multiplication rule," and it replaces a normal word with an out-of-place phrase. Also, it's kind of true.

3. A-1: The IDK stutter-step forces the speaker to switch up their speech patterns.

B-3: Speedy getaway is a great way for a teacher who is disliked to sound charmingly aloof.

C-2: Change the third item to something bad, and the usual telegraphing signs will become ironic instead of railroading.

REVIEW QUESTIONS: All Formulae

1. Which of the following situations is ripe for a forced transition? Choose all that apply:

A. Transitioning a bored high-school class from counting dots on the ceiling to a lecture about California's agricultural-based economy in the 1930s
B. A hyper elementary-school class that just got done with a "play games with a parachute" period
C. A high-school class abuzz about the apparent theft of 234 cases of ramen from the physics lab closet
D. A nursing school class that can't seem to stop chattering about a recent court ruling allowing extraterrestrials to vote in presidential elections
E. A teenage tutoring student who can't stop eating delicious spaghetti while Skyping with the instructor

2. All of these illustrate a successfully executed joke except:

A. "You know what else will be super scary tonight besides Halloween festivities? Not knowing how to successfully factor a polynomial!"

B. "There are three states of matter: solid, liquid, and Jell-O."

C. "You know what else amazing happened at lunch besides a helicopter throwing candy over the football field? An English professor prepping his lesson on Shakespeare. Turn to page 15."

D. "We'll be learning three basics of Spanish today: counting from 1 to 10, asking and saying our name, and screaming 'goooooooooooal' during overtime periods of World Cup soccer matches."

E. "A couple of cheerleaders, Mary and Quon-Lee, wore their outfits for spirit Friday. You know what they're thinking: Mark didn't wear a cheerleader outfit—why does Mark hate the football team?"

3. Which of these shows an effective schlemiel-schlimazel joke?

A. "Jim, your shoes are untied. I guess you're saying you're way cooler than Minnie, whose shoes don't even have laces."

B. "Bertrand, if you wear your hat in class, James, who took his hat off, is gonna feel disrespected."

C. "Jean-Luc, there are three things wrong with your coat: One, it's purple, and Harriet here hates purple. Two, it's a coat, and it's 70 degrees outside. And three, I can't mention enough about how much you are hating on Harriet."

D. "Who here thinks that Robert's unusual choice of backpack color is a shot against Marc's briefcase?"

E. "James, Gina, Tina Marie, Antonio, and Odysseus all have pencils, while Sean, Marcus, Tenille, and Aphrodite all have pens. Guess there's going to be a gang war over these differences!"

ANSWERS

1. C, D, and E involve a warm audience, which is 13+ years of age. The right ingredients.

   A is wrong because forced transitions aren't for cold audiences. Elementary schools are a little too young to notice the joke, which eliminates B.

2. D. The tempo is destroyed by the punch line being significantly longer than the first two items in the list. Had the punch line simply ended at "gooooooal," the joke would have landed.

3. For A, Minnie's shoes not having laces undermines the joke: she can't feel silly for not tying shoes that aren't tied. B has a schlemiel (Bertrand), a schlimazel (James), and an innocuous subject matter (general hat location). B is the correct answer. C is too long and unnecessarily merges two formats and keeps mentioning Harriet for some odd reason. Never prompt a cold audience for a response, like D does. E has a ridiculously overextended setup. Just say, "Rachel has a pen. James, you have a pencil—she's disrespecting your turf!"

Formula 4: Exaggeration
Target Audience: 5- to 18-Year-Olds
Cold/Warm Audience: Cold

It was a Sunday evening, around 6:00 p.m.. I was leading an SAT course with a group of about a dozen teens. I was happy to be there. For years, I had worked my way up the ladder at Kaplan by tutoring individual students (not my favorite job; I like to teach groups). Finally, I was put in charge of my first class. I'd say without a doubt that it was going... kind of good, I guess?

But today was different. Today was bordering on horrible, emphasis on horror, for the day was Halloween. My boss would later admit that someone made a big mistake scheduling a class on the evening of Halloween and that it was policy to not put classes around holidays.

So, naturally, the class was quite distracted. Phones were buzzing as they coordinated with their friends, and nobody could keep their mind on the SAT drills I had outlined on the board. Not only was I inexperienced with the class, no one should have to teach teenagers on Halloween night, so I had a unique situation on my hands that could go disastrously wrong if I didn't play things just right.

I decided Halloween night called for some terrifying tactics. I began a lengthy statement about the proper ways to break up a run-on sentence, but stopped suddenly in the middle. That got the attention of most of the class. Silently, but sternly, I gazed around the room. One by one, students looked up from their phones, confused, then alarmed. Finally all but one student was looking at the front of the room, all but one student was staring at me instead of at their screen.

"Kelsey!" I said, slightly loud and in a deep voice, "you're looking at your phone. That's punishable by hellfire."

Kelsey looked up, there were some giggles in the classroom.

"Or, since it's your first warning, you can just get up here and walk us through this verbal problem."

Kelsey came up to the front of the room. I stared at the class, "But for the rest of you," I lowered my voice to a whisper, "hellfire."

I turned to watch Kelsey demonstrate her problem. After about half a minute, in the middle of her speaking, I whirled around and shouted "HELLFIRE!" After the laughter had subsided, I called out the names of the students I had caught looking at their phone and made them demonstrate a problem in front of the class.

I didn't have any problems with the students making eye contact for the last hour, even when I had my back turned.

Now, of course, I'm not advocating you threaten hellfire to misbehaving students. I'll save that for a follow-up book called *Extremely Effective Teaching Methods*. In fact, as you can tell, exaggeration is a fine line to walk: you don't want your class to go home and tell their parents about how their instructor shouted hellfire threats at them. Or at least, I suspect you don't. I shouldn't tell you how to feel.

So the list of situations in which this is effective without risk of imploding on you is smaller than with the other joke types. Still, it is so effective when properly used that I'd be remiss to omit it.

The three situations where I have effectively used exaggeration to increase retention are:

1. When students are having extreme difficulties with a problem, and it's noticeably affecting their self-esteem

2. When I am having extreme difficulties with a class that is so frustrating I'm about to come unraveled

3. When I've got a long list of facts I need the students to remember

Let's unpack number 1 first because the number 1 comes first. There isn't much in the world more terrifyingly awkward than a student fumbling when called upon to answer a question. I used to dread standing there, having to gently coax each step out of shy students and hope they wouldn't break down. But now I love it because it's a great teaching opportunity to help a student build one of the most important life skills: maintaining composure when confronted with an impossible obstacle.

A bit of exaggeration humor is quite the tool here. First, take control of the situation and spin it positively, "I'm glad this is happening; we all have times when we don't immediately see the solution to the problem. Now, is Maddie here going to give up, run out of the class screaming, run on a bus (still screaming), run home, pack up her things, and join the circus? No, of course not… because circuses are cruel to animals, and Maddie's better than that."

I even wore a Halloween costume. I'm dressed as the monster known as "guy who thinks sweater vests are in fashion."

From there, people are laughing (for the right reason), the student has relaxed, and I can decide which teaching technique is best. Usually, I'll ask if anyone knows how to do the first step of the problem, then ask Maddie to call on someone, giving her a little bit of control over the situation. Hopefully, the next time she is anxious with a solve, she'll remember the exaggerated images of her screaming all the way across town, relax a bit, and also remember the feeling of control. I don't know really, I'm not about to author a book called *Teaching Using Feelings*. I'm just here to give you a brief bit of humor to keep the lesson on track and also replace feelings of dread and anxiety with something more conducive to retention.

QUESTION

Exactly one of these five situations is a prime instance for smoothing the situation over with some exaggeration. The other four are horribly, *horribly wrong*, and you should feel awful if you miss this. Just quit your career and exile yourself to the moon.

Which one of these is a good situation for using some exaggeration humor to smooth things over?

A. While attempting to recite the articles of the Bill of Rights, an 11-year-old's nose starts spontaneously bleeding.

B. After correctly answering a challenging question about conjugation, a French student adds "walla," utterly mispronouncing *voilà*.

C. Called upon to demonstrate factoring, a mousy high-school student begins to stutter.

D. The only male student in a cooking class is reciting a recipe. He mixes up teaspoons and tablespoons when describing how much salt to add. He corrects himself but then stops and blushes as several classmates giggle.

E. When called upon to explain the origin of the term *Dead Sea*, a student makes an embarrassing mispronunciation of "multiple organisms."

Answer: **D.** *The only male student in a cooking class is reciting a recipe. He mixes up teaspoons and tablespoons when describing how much salt to add. He corrects himself, but then stops and blushes as several classmates giggle.*

We've got a nervous student who doesn't know how to proceed, or is simply too scared to make another mistake. This is the perfect time to state, "Hey, everybody mixes up units. It could be worse—one time a recipe called for a pinch of yeast and I added a pint of yeast. The bread rose so much it spilled out of the oven and filled my entire house. Luckily, I was hungry or I would've been trapped in there forever. In your case, though, it would just make the final product a little more salty. Keep going!"

Use a little exaggeration to call attention away from the student's slightly embarrassing problem by describing an even more embarrassing problem. *Best of all, you don't have to worry about getting a laugh.* If the joke bombs, then it also takes the embarrassment away from the student and onto you.

Let's examine the other answers, which are wrong times to use exaggeration humor:

A. *While attempting to recite the articles of the Bill of Rights, an 11-year-old's nose starts spontaneously bleeding.*

The reason why we don't use exaggeration here is because the goal is no longer to encourage the student to keep going. The goal is to get the student medical attention to stop the nosebleed (in case you missed it, you sociopath) and refocus the class's attention back to the lesson.

B. *After correctly answering a challenging question about conjugation, a French student adds "walla," utterly mispronouncing* voilà.

We don't want to use humor here because the student has already confidently solved the problem. A simple correction won't hurt their self-esteem or retention, especially if couched in praise. "It's pronounced *voilà*, but everything else you said was absolutely correct," is good enough to keep the lesson moving. Plus, your student already did your job as a comedian for you, as classmates who noticed the funny pronunciation are more likely to remember the correction.

C. *Called upon to demonstrate factoring, a mousy high-school student begins to stutter.*

This can sometimes be a land mine. If the stutter is an actual physical disability rather than a brief nervous tic, then no amount of exaggeration will get them back on track. You can figure this out by giving the student the chance to bow out, asking, "Would you like to sit down and write this one out, and we'll get back to you?" Then later, you can privately ask the student if it was nerves or a more pronounced impairment that hindered the student's ability to answer a question.

E. *When called upon to explain the origin of the term* Dead Sea, *a student makes an embarrassing mispronunciation of "multiple organisms."*

No need to try to make a joke here, a hilarious gaffe has already hit the airwaves. Get the class back on track by being as mundane as possible: "Correct! Although the Dead Sea's water is too salty for larger creatures, there are fungi and bacteria that live there." You can rest assured that no one in the class is going to forget that fact after such an attention-grabbing setup, if they hear it over the laughter.

As you can see, it's quite simple: if a student is struggling with a problem due to a lack of confidence, an exaggeration joke usually lands (and if it doesn't land, it still takes the focus off them). Otherwise, the only good times for an exaggeration joke are with an especially difficult class or for spicing up a long, boring list of facts. More on those instances later, but first let's round out using exaggeration to put students' nerves at ease by having you practice making some jokes yourself.

The following three situations are prime opportunities for making an exaggeration-based joke to keep the lesson moving and increase retention. Brainstorm at least two different jokes you could make, then check the answers to see what I came up with:

1. When called upon to answer "What is 5 times 7?" a seven-year-old second grader screams, "I don't want to do it!"

2. Asked to list the steps in the scientific method, a trembling middle-school student stops talking halfway through and says "ummmm" for 10 straight seconds.

3. In a technology-driven future, you are leading a clone programming seminar. A clone of an important client forgets the middle name of his brother and begins to cry.

ANSWERS

(Naturally, there's not a set list of answers that work for these. There are infinite good jokes that can be made. Just make sure your jokes are inoffensive and don't highlight the mistake, but instead make it seem insignificant.)

1. *When called upon to answer "What is 5 times 7?" a seven-year-old second grader screams, "I don't want to do it!"*

With smaller children, it's important to demonstrate making an even bigger mistake. There's a reason why clowns are popular with small children despite terrifying everyone else—little children love seeing adults mess up their lives. Yes, I have an extremely sad take on the role of clowns, but that's not important.

I find the most success simply outlining the first steps and then making a huge mistake. For instance, I might say, "That's okay. I never want to do math problems, nobody does. Just count by 5s, like this: 5; 10; 15; 20; 16,000,000; 300,000; 451." At this point, at least one of the children will correct me. Hopefully it will be the child that is demonstrating the problem. Let's call him David.

If someone else answers, I steer it back to David. "Oh, what comes next? Twenty-five, huh? Is that right, David? What's next after that?"

Alternately, I could steer them toward process of elimination. "Is the answer... SIX BILLION? Why not? It's too high, right?" Building confidence in young children, as any elementary-school teacher knows, takes small steps. Once we've got them back on track and increased their confidence a little, we could narrow it down. "What if the choices were 34, 35, or 36... what then?"

2. *Asked to list the steps in the scientific method, a trembling middle-school student stops talking halfway through, and says "ummmm" for 10 straight seconds.*

For an exaggeration joke to really hit, we need to focus on what the problem is trying to avoid... what the opposite of the right answer is. In the 5 times 7 problem, the right answer is a little number, so a huge number becomes a stark exaggeration. For the scientific method, the purpose is to find an empirical way to test out different ways that might solve a problem. So the absolute wrong answer will not solve the problem, not address the problem, make the problem worse, or introduce more problems.

Let's say the student (we'll call her Zoe) is stuck at remembering step three of the scientific method. I find a lot of students get stuck here because they have trouble remembering the word *hypothesis*. *Hypothesis* is a good word to know, but it's not necessary when memorizing the parts of the scientific method. If we separate the problem into two parts, *What are we doing?* and *What is it called?*, the problem becomes easier. I often tell the students to picture three boxes filled with coins: a small box, a medium box, and a large box. I tell them to pretend they are in a contest where if they pick the box with the highest value of money in it, they win the money.

"Do we know which of the boxes has the most money? What if the two larger boxes have pennies and the smaller box has $20 gold coins? What if it's stuffed with gold coins: you open the side and a river of gold coins comes flowing out? That's right, we don't know. So do we refuse to answer, throw ourselves on the ground, and curl up into a ball? No? What would you do?"

The student invariably answers, "Make a guess" or "Guess the largest box."

"Great, step three is a guess. Only scientists can't call it a guess or people will think they're clueless. So they call it a hypothesis."

Sometimes they forget step five: analysis. This is, in my opinion, not only the most critical step of the scientific method, but one of the most important lessons we can teach young adults. While it is intuitive to many adults, a high percentage of people when presented with a bunch of data will choose the answer they originally wanted to be correct, then select the data that supports their conclusion. It's why we can't have actual debates about what sports team is the best, or differences in religions, or which politician to vote for. People have it ingrained in them that one way is the correct way, so they will always cite statistics and facts that support the way they believe. It leads to a giant echo chamber and is the reason why we never make any progress in religious or political tolerance (or, I guess, sports tolerance, although that rarely leads to war outside of a bar setting).

When a student gets tripped up after the experiment step, I love telling them, "Okay. Pretend we have those three boxes of coins. You chose the largest one because your theory is that it probably has the most money. Then we experiment by counting up the money. What then? Do we just look at the amount of money we totaled for the largest box and go, 'Yep, that's the right answer because it sure is a lot of money,' then go out and buy ourselves a humongous gold belt that says *World Champion of Money Box Guessing*?"

Naturally, I'm spoon-feeding them the answer, but I'm (hopefully) doing it in a way that increases retention through humor and visuals. Inevitably, the student will respond, "No, we have to compare the amount of money in the large box to the other two boxes." Walla! We have changed the thought processes of the next generation, opening up our society for much more harmonious conflict resolution. We have saved the entire world!

Yes, I used exaggeration there to increase your retention of this lesson. Yes, you should feel condescended to, and you should get angry. Seriously, we're like halfway through a workbook here, but we're at some of the most critical lessons. I can't have you drifting off—even if it means kickstarting your brain with adrenaline by filling you with rage!

NOTE: Inciting your students to a frothing rage is not a good tool for increasing student retention.

3. *In a technology-driven future, you are leading a clone-programming seminar. A clone of an important client forgets the middle name of his brother and begins to cry.*

Look, I don't know whether this book is going to be on shelves a few dozen years into the future. I don't even know if we will have shelves or if stores will just have books levitating with, like, jetpacks or whatever.

I only know that by then, the world will probably be populated mostly by clones because they will be so easy to make. So I'm betting on increasing book sales in the year 2030 by dropping some clone-applicable learning. It still has useful information for today's classrooms, so pay attention.

Whether we're talking about clones in the future or simply a rundown of client characteristics before a sales meeting, middle names aren't that important. So a decent exaggeration joke will overstate the importance of them. "Okay, so you can't remember your brother's middle name; what if you guessed that it was 'Jupiter's largest moon, Titania, also known as B-4594'? That's right, you would out yourself as a clone and be arrested and sentenced to a lifetime of forced labor in the binary mines." (Note, for this example, you have to pretend that the future has a shortage of the numbers one and zero.) "What's a better answer? That's right, a normal name, or just say you forgot. Humans forget each other's middle names all the time because we don't use them on a day-to-day basis." Note how I'm also throwing in some good facts about humans, since my joke has gotten their memory circuits adequately stimulated.

I don't actually need to come up with a second joke here. The good news about clones is that the same joke works on every copy of them.

Another common way to derail a class is to describe long lists of facts or mundane historical events. Solid teachers find ways to break these up whenever possible, but sometimes you just don't have enough time to weave a list around an entire lesson plan. Exaggeration is a great way to transform a boring patch of rote memorization into something that will make students lean forward.

Take this excerpt, which I paraphrased from a source that was either a peer-reviewed history book or Wikipedia:

In 911 AD, the Carolingian ruler Charles let the Vikings settle in Normandy. After a while, these Vikings blended in with the local culture. They married among the population that had been there and converted to Christianity.

In 1002 AD, King Æthelred II married the Duke of Normandy's sister, Emma. Their son, Edward the Confessor, got exiled from Normandy for a while and then became king in 1042.

Part of the reason why history gets so boring, even though it can be one of the most fascinating subjects, is that it takes so long for the action to set up. These preceding paragraphs are only about one-fifth of the setup my source uses before it finally gets to the Battle of Hastings and all the excitement detailed within. It's like if a movie just kept introducing new characters for an hour before finally having people actually doing stuff in the final act. It's not the students' fault that they have low retention rates for this kind of stuff—they get buried under a landslide of facts without knowing which ones are most important to the action that will eventually unfurl.

So what facts are most important as a general rule of thumb? For the majority of students, history plays no direct part in their future careers, so why is it a fundamental subject of modern US public-school curriculums?

We learn history because it exposes us to the ramifications of the decisions of past cultures. No one knows for sure what decisions will best shape our current societal landscapes (except that buying my books is mandatory for a bright future), but we can sure get a good idea by looking at the past. That way, we can avoid doing things like punishing the loser of a war in such an economically exacting way that they have no way to get out of their debts besides...starting another war.

Of course, since you're probably a teacher, you already knew that... I can work with that.

You want to keep the students alert while you set the scene elaborately so when you finally get to the good stuff, they are riveted by the amazing power of historical anecdotes. Then no doubt they will go on to lead their nation into uncharted heights.

Or they just pay attention until the bell rings. Either way is good.

Let's punch things up with a little exaggeration:

In 911 AD, the Carolingian ruler Charles let the Vikings settle in Normandy.

"Would you let a bunch of uncouth Vikings set up in a corner of your bedroom? Of course not, but this is almost exactly what Charles did: he let a group known for their savagery just come on in and mingle with his precious kingdom. This was a very interesting development that would have ramifications throughout the discovered world."

After a while, these Vikings blended in with the local culture. They married among the population that had been there and converted to Christianity.

"Think about that. In the history of the world, Vikings have to be close to number one in terms of being known for wild, aggressive behavior, right behind the Mongols and just ahead of my kids. Yet even they grew to fit in. So there's still hope for some of you."

In 1002 AD, King Æthelred II married the Duke of Normandy's sister, Emma.

"He had a lot to offer, such as the super rare and extremely powerful knowledge of how to use this crazy new letter, Æ."

Their son, Edward the Confessor, got exiled from Normandy for a while and then became king in 1042.

"That's one of the greatest turnarounds in history. Hey, I'm banned from Normandy... fast-forward a bit, aaaaand now I'm King of Normandy. He showed great self-control in not vengefully banning everyone else but himself from the country immediately, which is what I would've done."

You don't want to put in exaggeration jokes as frequently as I have here; usually only one or two every couple of paragraphs is enough to keep most students absorbing the information.

QUESTION

Which joke is most likely to increase retention of the following fact: *From 1977 to 2011, the flag of Libya was solid green.*

A. "From 1977 to 2011, the flag of Libya was solid green, and it was perpetually on fire due to national law!"
B. "From 1977 to 2011, the president of Libya said, 'Hurrah, the most exciting flag is solid green! I'm boring!'"
C. "From 1977 to 2011, the flag of Libya was the boldest, brightest, most intense shade of green. Green like the brightest traffic light in the world. Like, if the sun were a lime, that's how green!"
D. "Half the people wanted Libya's flag to be blue, half wanted it to be yellow. So they settled on green!"
E. "From 1977 to 2011, Libya had the most wacky, extreme flag design of all time: solid green!"

Answer: **C.** *"From 1977 to 2011, the flag of Libya was the boldest, brightest, most intense shade of green. Green like the brightest traffic light in the world. Like if the sun were a lime, that's how green!"*

C takes the boring fact (a solid green flag) and blows it up. It also uses imagery (lime, traffic light) to cement the color in students' minds.

WRONG ANSWERS

A. *"From 1977 to 2011, the flag of Libya was solid green, and it was perpetually on fire due to national law!"*

This is kind of wacky, but the "on fire" fact doesn't do anything to link to the color green. In fact, fire is not green (unless, of course, the flag was made of boron), so the analogy might conflate colors in the students' memory.

B. *"From 1977 to 2011, the president of Libya said, 'Hurrah, the most exciting flag is solid green! I'm boring!'"*

This is unnecessarily mean. Calling the leader of a country inept isn't the right statement for a teacher to make. That's an important tip in general: don't go too far into the negative or extreme when doing impressions.

D. *"Half the people wanted Libya's flag to be blue, half wanted it to be yellow. So they settled on green!"*

This doesn't exaggerate anything. It also presents two other colors, which is easy to jumble up in the mind of an uninterested student (or me, frankly—I just don't care about flags).

E. *"From 1977 to 2011, Libya had the most wacky, extreme flag design of all time: solid green!"*

This is actually a 180-degree turn. Most people don't realize it, but every sarcastic remark is a 180-degree-turn joke. You set up a statement that seems to go one way (exciting flag), then take it the other way (boring flag). It's a joke, sure, but facts shouldn't have reverse-facts preceding them that can cause confusion and conflicting ideas when a student tries to retrieve the knowledge. 180s aren't great for fact retention.

QUESTION

Read the factual statement below and then choose the joke that will most likely cement the fact into the mind of a student:

In 1963, the Studebaker auto plant in South Bend, Indiana, closed down.

A. "In 1963, the Studebaker auto plant in South Bend, Indiana, known for making the worst cars on the planet, closed down."

B. "In 1963, the Studebaker auto plant in South Bend, Indiana, closed down. For over 50 years, the giant tower of the auto-making plant has loomed over the town of South Bend like a six-story-tall billboard declaring, 'You can't find jobs here!'"

C. "In 1963, the Studebaker auto plant in South Bend, Indiana, closed down. South Bend was no longer the greatest city on the planet."

D. "In 1963, a million years ago when the dinosaurs ruled the earth, the Studebaker auto plant in South Bend, Indiana, closed down."

E. "In 1963, the Studebaker auto plant in South Bend, Indiana, closed down FOREVER!"

First, we need to determine what info we want the students to retain. It's that about 50 years ago, a major auto manufacturer in a rural town closed, crushing the local economy. Now let's examine each answer, starting with the correct one...

Answer: **B.** *"In 1963, the Studebaker auto plant in South Bend, Indiana, closed down. For over 50 years, the giant tower of the automaking plant has loomed over the town of South Bend like a six-story-tall billboard declaring, 'You can't find jobs here!'"*

B is correct. Note how it's barely a joke. The huge building really is a looming six-story-tall reminder of how there used to be a lot more jobs. When I'm having trouble making a joke, I often ask myself, "What is the deeper meaning I want the students to realize?" The humor usually flows from there. If it doesn't, no problem—not everything needs to be a joke. What's more important is that we make these facts meaningful; the gutted Studebaker plant has been a constant, painful reminder to citizens of South Bend that change happened and hurt the job market.

Using this platitude ("attach meaning to facts"), we can re-examine the previous question: From 1977 to 2011, Libya's flag was solid green to symbolize Islam and the *Green Book* their leader published to copy Mao's *Little Red Book*. Hey, that's kinda funny without embellishment: he took someone's book color and changed it to ride that wave of popularity.

Bringing meaning to facts increases retention. Since this doesn't fall under comedy, I won't mention it again, but it's a great teaching tool.

A. *"In 1963, the Studebaker auto plant in South Bend, Indiana, known for making the worst cars on the planet, closed down."*

Be careful before insulting anything. While this comment probably isn't going to offend anyone, it brings a negativity into the classroom that is hard to work with. Plus, it doesn't really reflect what we're trying to teach. The car quality is not situationally relevant to the closing of a huge factory. Situationally relevant humor is the Holy Grail of comedy writing. It's the origin of the word *sitcom* (situational comedy). Retention best happens when the jokes reflect the greater workings and influences of the event rather than simple wordplay or goofiness.

C. *"In 1963, the Studebaker auto plant in South Bend, Indiana, closed down. South Bend was no longer the greatest city on the planet."*

It's probably becoming much more clear now: the greatness of South Bend, while exaggerated correctly, is not important. What is important is that it went from a great producer of auto-related jobs to having none of these jobs. If you wanted to add "South Bend was no longer a great producer of auto-related jobs," that's excellent—not everything needs to be a joke.

D. *"In 1963, a million years ago when the dinosaurs ruled the earth, the Studebaker auto plant in South Bend, Indiana, closed down."*

Again, this is not situationally relevant, but I designed it to illustrate an even more dangerous trap. These facts are difficult to remember and retain because they don't seem relevant to students. What does a 1963 auto-plant closure have to do with any aspect of modern life? Exaggerating how long ago the event happened makes it even more unrelatable. This has an opposite effect on retention.

E. *In 1963, the Studebaker auto plant in South Bend, Indiana, closed down FOREVER!*

Again, this is not the situation the statement is trying to convey. We don't know that it's forever. The city of South Bend is constantly trying to repurpose the building. Whenever possible, we want to minimize the risk that students will confuse an exaggeration with a true fact.

Another situation that finds me leaning on exaggeration is when I'm extremely frustrated with my class. Ninety percent of the time this happens with middle-school students (12 to 14 years old). Oh, that sweet middle-school time, when all the students are coming to grips with their newfound powers to defy authority. The key is not to be angry when I punish students. They'll see that I'm vulnerable and run straight into that weak spot. So to maintain control while still being discipline-focused, I find it best to use exaggeration.

Another reason why I want to focus on worst-case middle-school class scenarios is that due to the nature of my job, I almost exclusively encountered classes at their worst. This is because I've only subbed for middle school, and we all know how a substitute can be a great excuse for students to act up. I know I was on my worst behavior whenever we had a substitute (as opposed to my normal, excessively-bad-but-not-worst behavior when we had the regular teacher).

When one internet-searches for tips about substitute teaching middle school, nearly half of them are "Be strict with all the rules." Normally, this would be a resounding endorsement of rigid behavior except that the other half of the tips are "Be loose and friendly." Why is there such a polarity in opinion? To get to the bottom of this, I stared deep into the black void of my soul that is "memories from when I was in middle school." I realized three things:

1. Whenever we had a sub who was a strict rules follower, it made me want to push their limits to see where their boundaries were. And I tried move those boundaries with sheer force of will. I don't know, I was bored a lot.

2. Whenever we had a sub who was friendly and sociable, it made me want to slack off and rebel. Middle school was stressful for me, as was home life. I took any opportunity I could to blow off that stress.

3. No matter what the sub did, I looked for an excuse to misbehave.

There was no magic bullet substitute personality that made me want to settle down. It was their actions, not their persona or jokes, that got me to behave. Teachers that came in and established clear guidelines for punishment, then enforced those guidelines, were the ones who had the most success.

This might lead you to wonder if there is any room for jokemaking for middle-school substitute teachers. The answer is "yes," and not just because I have to fill out a few hundred more words in this chapter. The key is retention. If you learn only one thing from this book, then, wow, you need to work on your reading comprehension skills. Maybe take my Kaplan course. But the main thing I want all teachers to take from this book is that jokes should only be used to increase student retention.

So what do teachers, especially substitutes, want their middle-school pupils to retain? There are rules and punishments that will be enforced. Students have short attention spans, so a good joke can help them retain the notion that, yes, they will be punished in a quantifiable way if they act out.

How do we do that? How do we blend in a retention-facilitating joke while still making sure students are taking the rules seriously? I find an exaggeration joke to be the best tool in this situation.

A lot of teachers like to exaggerate how bad the punishment will be. "If you talk out of turn once, you will lose five points off your overall grade. If you talk out of turn twice, I will SCREAM AT YOU AND MAKE YOU DEMONSTRATE TWO WORD PROBLEMS!"

I hear good results from this, so if it's something you were thinking of doing, go for it. It's not for me, though. Teaching is my fun job; my 9–5, M–F job is banging my head against the wall trying to think of jokes, then bothering my friends at their 9–5, M–F jobs by asking "IS THIS FUNNY?" I'm social, though: I like a crowd, I like a challenge, and I like public speaking.

Growing up, I had a speech impediment that was indirectly linked to my ADHD. When I was a student, they hadn't invented non-stimulant ADHD medication. At least I think they hadn't; I'm not going to research it because it won't help me explain jokemaking. Anyway, the preferred treatment for ADHD was to stimulate the gland that produces attention juice in the human body (again, not going to research science words). That helps the symptoms, but giving a stimulant to someone who is already extremely hyperactive sometimes has the unintended side effect of making them speak like a strung-out meth head. So for the formative years of my childhood, every time I had a right answer or a creative solution to a problem, I struggled to slow down enough for anyone to understand what I was saying.

So now that I'm an adult and I have everything straightened out, I can talk in a calm and rational manner in all situations (except disciplining my own kids, a situation that frequently finds me losing my mind). I teach for fun.

You might think that's a cheap way to get a captive audience without actually crafting a speech that earns respect. Maybe.

You might think this is a desperate way to recapture self-esteem I lost as a tween. Probably.

You might not have expected the author of a comedy-writing book to be a somewhat broken person. Okay, that one's on *you*.

The point is, I don't like to come across as mean. This is a job I do to relax while explaining complex concepts in ways that maximize retention. So I have no interest in creating a mean persona, even if it is the most surefire way to tamp down the antics of a middle-school class. I developed a different kind of exaggeration joke that increases the chances of the students remembering that, yes, I am in charge and, yes, there are consequences. It goes like this:

"My name is Mr. Hoovler and I am in charge today. In my class, there is only one rule...and that one rule is that THERE ARE EXACTLY THREE RULES. First, if you talk out of turn, it's five points off. Second, if you need to talk or do anything, you must always raise your hand and wait to be called on. Third, I will make a note if anything goes poorly and give it to your regular teacher so they can handle discipline in their usual way.

The "exactly three rules" bit always gets a laugh and helps the students remember that there are rules and consequences without making myself seem like too much of a bad guy. Note that when you say "There is only one rule," about half the time a student will shout out, "And that rule is that there are no rules!" Allow a pause for that and any subsequent laughter. It's good—the sudden transition between the student shouting that there are no rules and your displaying that there are actually more rules than previously stated is stark enough to boost the power of the joke.

Question time!

QUESTION

It is the first day of your middle-school class. This question applies to both substitute teachers and regular teachers, so let's just say you can't remember whether you are a substitute or not. Armed with Evan Hoovler's powerful joke teachings, you are confident that you will rein them in with only a few short sentences. "Welcome, class," you say, almost giddy with the opportunity to make them laugh and learn. "There is only one rule..."

"And that is that I am in charge!" barks a student from the back. He stands up, wearing the colorful red-and-yellow leather outfit worn by the school's currently reigning tribe.

(Oh, by the way, this is postapocalyptic. Did I mention that? It's important.)

Anyway, the student pulls out an electric guitar that doubles as a taser that he cobbled together in metal shop. He eyes you challengingly.

This doesn't faze you; you knew the job would be difficult when you saw the display of former teachers' heads impaled upon spikes outside the classroom door. Confidently, you step toward the tribal representative and say...

Jokemaking Techniques Workbook | 71

A. "It is I, the chosen one of prophecy. I have traveled many moons and endured a multitude of catastrophes just to bring you this message from your one true god: if you have to go to the bathroom, raise your hand and wait to be called on!"

B. "That is an amazing electric guitaser gun. Can I see it?"

C. "Your taser-tar has no effect on me, as I am wearing special antigrounding boots. Five points off. Now come up here and solve this right-triangle diagram in front of the class!"

D. "Your electaser guitar is pathetic. We shall do battle! For my weapon, I choose...that thing that lets music teachers hold five pieces of chalk!"

E. "And that rule is that THERE ARE EXACTLY THREE RULES! Rule one: If you talk out of turn, you lose five points. Second, if you need to talk or do anything, you must always raise your hand and wait to be called on. Third, I make a chalk etching of anyone who gets points off just in case you give me a fake name. These etchings and points off will be sent to your regular teacher, and then I will burn them in that giant bonfire in the middle of the quad."

Answer: **E.** *"And that rule is that THERE ARE EXACTLY THREE RULES! Rule one: If you talk out of turn, you lose five points. Second, if you need to talk or do anything, you must always raise your hand and wait to be called on. Third, I make a chalk etching of anyone who gets points off just in case you give me a fake name. These etchings and points off will be sent to your regular teacher, and then I will burn them in that giant bonfire in the middle of the quad."*

It doesn't matter what middle schoolers do, we all know the old adage that students frequently misbehave to get attention. Just like you should continue on if a student screams, "And that rule is that there are no rules," you should show no acknowledgement of a student who wields a ridiculous weapon that probably doesn't even work. These are students, and acknowledging them only gives them power.

Let's take a look at why each of the wrong answers are incorrect and will probably lead to the early retirement of your spine's C1 vertebra:

A. *"It is I, the chosen one of prophecy. I have traveled many moons and endured a multitude of catastrophes just to bring you this message from your one true god: if you have to go to the bathroom, raise your hand and wait to be called on!"*

First of all, don't bring religion into the classroom; that is a basic rule. Second, this is a great escalation needed for an exaggeration joke...actually, yeah, this is a great way for them to learn that hand-raising is mandatory for speaking. Just take out the theological stuff and you're good.

B. *"That is an amazing electric guitaser gun. Can I see it?"*

Even if this ruse succeeds in disarming the tribe leader, you can rest assured it's not the only weapon in class. The tweenage cult has no doubt spent most of recess fashioning incredibly elaborate and dangerous weapons out of their fastidiously maintained collection of recommended school supplies.

C. *"Your taser-tar has no effect on me, as I am wearing special antigrounding boots. Five points off. Now come up here and solve this right-triangle diagram in front of the class!"*

Okay, for starters, don't call your rubber-soled shoes "special antigrounding boots"—you sound pompous. Second, while you may be impervious to the taser end of the weapon, no special boot material will protect you from a roundhouse guitar delivered to your face by a middle-school student who is simultaneously hammering the solo to a Frank Zappa song (probably "Muffin Man"). The real-life translation of this advice is, "Don't overtly state that a student's callout doesn't bother you."

D. *"Your electaser guitar is pathetic. We shall do battle! For my weapon, I choose…that thing that lets music teachers hold five pieces of chalk!"*

Three things: One, the tool that lets music teachers hold five pieces of chalk is called a "quintoscribe." Two, you can't possibly defeat a tribal leader and still have enough time left to adequately explain and demonstrate the Pythagorean theorem to an already-distracted class. Sci-fi satire aside, teachers have a lot of information to give in a fixed amount of time. Three, the thing that holds five pieces of chalk is not called a "quintoscribe." I just made that up because it is not my job to Google obscure teaching supplies.

Formula 5: Repetition
Age Group: All
Cold/Warm Audience: Cold

Of all the subjects I've taught, there's none I enjoy more than teaching future lawyers ways to improve their scores on the LSAT, the law-school standardized test. These students, the future lawyers of America, are challenging, demanding, and assertive. Give me a class where people constantly question everything I say over a class where everyone just sits there. Sure, it's way more challenging for me, I often don't have immediate answers, and frankly, there's a lot of fighting, screaming, and even crying (and sometimes the students get emotional too). But that keeps everyone awake. LSAT students frequently have the highest jump in scores of any of my Kaplan classes. This isn't because I know literally anything about law, but because they are leaning forward throughout the entire arduous four-hour marathon of each class.

Okay, anecdote time, prepare for italics... now!

It took all of my comedy-generating resources when I was faced with an LSAT class that wasn't energized. It's not like the students were lazy or unmotivated. They were just as compelled to learn as students from any other LSAT class. They were so driven that they had already worked long days at their jobs before starting my 6:00 p.m.–9:00 p.m. class. They were simply tired, and the last two hours of class were an exercise in mental exhaustion. By 9:00 p.m., the students couldn't do simple things, such as recite the methods they were using on each and every problem. Their brains were zapped.

I usually don't make humor the forefront of my lessons. By now you have probably realized that even more important than a good joke is the ability to recognize the many, many times when a joke is riskier than the reward it may deliver. But this was different, I needed to keep these adult students' brains sizzling for four consecutive hours.

The transition from the outside world to the classroom was the first junction where I needed to reach these students. They were tired from working hard jobs, and it would be easy for them to slump into their class chairs and zone out for a few hours. I needed to stop that, and I needed to do it with a joke that required a minimum amount of concentration to comprehend.

That's actually easier than you might think: the more brain-zonked someone is, the less care you should put into creating an amazing joke. Hundreds of sitcoms have used this formula to entertain the tired and overworked, much to the anger of internet nerds who get super enraged that the number-one sitcom is about, say, a magic toilet company that only needs scatological puns to fix plumbing issues.

Simple repetition is all it really takes. When a student came into the LSAT class, I'd say their name and then a simple pleasantry. "Hey, Dionne, how are you? That's good. I'm fine. I hope it doesn't rain tonight so I can go hunt Pokémon with my kids."

That's it. Notice how it's not even a joke at all, just me making a simple pleasantry to engage the student as they walked in. Here's the trick: students didn't come into the room all at once; they trickled in one or two at a time over the half hour before class started. So each time someone came in, I'd say, "Hey, how are you? That's good. I'm fine. I hope it doesn't rain tonight so I can go hunt Pokémon with my kids."

"Hey, how are you? That's good. I'm fine. I hope it doesn't rain tonight so I can go hunt Pokémon with my kids."

"Hey, how are you? That's good. I'm fine. I hope it doesn't rain tonight so I can go hunt Pokémon with my kids."

Pretty quickly, the class recognizes the pattern, and the statement somehow becomes hilariously ludicrous each time it is repeated. It's like when you say a word to yourself over and over until it loses its meaning. After that, you can elicit laughter simply by breaking up the tempo and changing a few words:

"Hey, how are you? That's good. I'm fine. [look at the class, shrug] I still hope it doesn't rain tonight so I can go hunt Pokémon with my kids."

"Hey, how are you? That's good. I'm…[shrug, look at the class] still fine. Hope it doesn't rain tonight so I can go hunt Pokémon with my kids."

It might not translate to the written page, but everyone in class was laughing, even though I really hadn't made any jokes or effort at all. Establishing a pattern and then changing that pattern is classic low-process comedy. It got students paying attention before class, eager to see what I would utter when a new student came in. I had gotten them through the transition from work to class without losing their alertness. And it was easy to segue right into my lesson when the last student came in:

"Hey, how are you? That's good…"

[Long pause. Everyone is waiting for me to mention Pokémon hunting with my kids. They are alert and paying attention. My job is done. Time for my real job—teaching a class.]

"I'm cool. Our lesson today focuses on logical reasoning. Open your books to page 179…"

Repetition is so simple that most of the focus of this section will be on recognizing when not to use it. It's like when I give my kids a new toy they are super excited about, and within one day they will get in trouble for misusing it: taking it to school, throwing it at each other, fighting over it, etc. That's not to say that you, my cherished readers, are juvenile. My readers are erudite, demure, and (most importantly) have money to blow on a great book.

Repetition is like that new toy for most aspiring jokemakers. It's so simple, you'll want to use it throughout every class. But that will lead to disaster.

First and foremost, repetition jokes take a lot of time. Note that my successful application of the repetition to get my LSAT class motivated took *half an hour*! If I had tried something like that during class, I'm sure I would have gotten no laughs and probably a lot of complaints from impatient students who paid a lot of money to learn about the LSAT, not hear semiconstructed humor techniques.

Second, there's a big risk in simply repeating the same thing over and over. Alert students will zone out rather than laugh. Congrats, we just turned an alert student into an inattentive one, the opposite of what we're supposed to be doing.

So there's a high risk when it comes to both efficiency and retention.

That's why you need to only use a repetition joke when two conditions occur: you have a very inattentive class and you have time to deliver the joke that won't cut away from actual lesson time. Obviously, doing this before class is a great window for trying it. But I definitely couldn't deliver this to my high-school classes or when I'm teaching five-year-olds to do something because they tend to all come in at once or in large groups.

I don't hunt Pokémon with my kids anymore.
These days, we just hire an exterminator.

Workbook Activity

Below are 10 classroom setups. Choose the ones where a repetition joke most likely has more reward than risk:

1. A preschool class is sitting down, but inattentive after someone brings in sugar cookies for snack time. You are tasked with focusing them to learn animal sounds.

2. A three-hour graduate-school entrance examination (GMAT) class is frustrated with perceived logical inconsistencies about inference-based reading comprehension questions.

3. During a freak thunderstorm, a 50-minute middle-school social-studies class has become convinced that a series of weird noises coming from the walls means the classroom is haunted.

4. A bunch of corporate trainees taking a day-long business ethics course are preoccupied with planning their postclass golf outing.

5. A substitute elementary-school music teacher is having trouble getting the choir to harmonize on high C.

6. On the first day of clown college, a lecture on the history of oversized bow ties keeps getting derailed by a rowdy class of students who won't stop honking their red noses.

7. A double-period high-school English class is distracted after a student has an epileptic seizure and is taken to the hospital.

8. A half-day kindergarten class is in tears after a student spread false rumors at recess that they would all get to watch a popular animated movie starring a sentient toothbrush who discovers there's a cavity… in his soul.

9. A freak windstorm has knocked out the power to your seventh-grade pre-algebra class, and students are restless because they aren't allowed to leave until the lights come back on or their parents pick them up.

10. Your four-hour LSAT prep class hasn't gotten a question right in 20 minutes. Even basic, obvious ones. They are tired.

ANSWERS

1. *A preschool class is sitting down, but inattentive after someone brings in sugar cookies for snack time. You are tasked with focusing them to learn animal sounds.*

Yes. The two ingredients are there: an unfocused class and plenty of time (because it's not like preschool is a tightly controlled, learning-intensive deal).

There is so much in the world of communication that goes over young children's heads that "getting" a joke is of great interest to them. I've had to lead playgroups of 7 to 10 toddlers and, when it comes to getting them on track, nothing gets them more focused than picking up an animal and saying, "The [animal] goes meee-ow."

Well, that's not true—nothing gets tots more focused than a practiced and drilled melodic saying ("1-2-3…eyes on me"). But if you don't know what the class call-and-response phrases are, you'll have to resort to humor. Once you've engaged their focus with one of these simple sayings, retain it with a good repetition joke. Pick up the toy horse and say, "The horse goes meee-ow." This should elicit some giggles and correction, and now the ball is rolling. Pick up a toy dog and say, "Okay, the dog goes meee-ow, then?" Get increasingly frustrated. I'm sure I'm not telling you anything you don't already know—getting kids engaged with laughter is simple.

So don't let the joke go on longer than it needs to. Two to three repetitions should be enough to get all or most of the students focused on the lesson. Too much repetition can convey the message that being silly is okay. A joke should be used like a doctor uses a pen to do an emergency tracheotomy: it's great when you need to get an out-of-control situation back in a pinch, but if you use it too much in your day-to-day job, you'll get slapped with a malpractice suit (they have those in teaching, right?).

Be careful! These children were already sitting, just inattentive. In contrast, a rowdy mob of toddlers is rife with kinetic energy just waiting to erupt and create an all-out distraction. Obviously, maintaining control is key, so focus on that before making the jokes. If you are in charge of preschoolers, you hopefully have learned the tools to get them at least settled, if not focused. Use those to regain control first, worry about delivering a joke later.

2. *A three-hour graduate-school entrance examination (GMAT) class is frustrated with perceived logical inconsistencies about inference-based reading comprehension questions.*

Yes. The class is distracted by doubt, and you have enough time.

One of my favorite things about the GMAT entrance exam for postgraduate business school is that it really reflects the learning that students will need to succeed in business, much more so than other standardized examinations. (Why does everyone getting a master's degree in an art/humanities need to take the GRE, which is half comprised of math?)

One of the key skills in business is figuring out exactly what your clients want. I've owned small businesses before, and one of the most common errors I made starting out was giving my potential clients something that was perfectly designed to suit their needs, but not perfectly designed to give them what they wanted.

This seems counterintuitive at first, especially for the usual black-and-white spreadsheet-oriented thinkers that take the GMAT, but it's key. For example, from a pragmatic standpoint, pretend you own a car dealership. Now, nearly every car shopper can optimally benefit from a well-built, long-lasting, two-year-old car that has depreciated significantly but still has 10–15 years ahead of it. But many car shoppers don't want that. They want a sports car or a car that looks tough or a car they can fit 42 of their friends into for commuting to clown college. If you offer those people a "very pragmatic" car, they'll never buy and you'll go bankrupt.

The key is to infer what your customer wants, then offer that to them.

This is why the GMAT tests for inference: it's better to read a client than to memorize and recite a spreadsheet. Getting that into my students' heads is understandably difficult. They have to learn what the test maker wants them to say, which is often not logically optimal. As such, I've come to lean upon a repetition-based joke that seems to resonate with these business-oriented students:

"You own a sandwich shop," I explain. "Obviously increasing bottom line is your goal, but reading your client takes practice. Let's say someone named Silent Steve comes in and, not being able to speak a word, points to his knee. Obviously, you could offer him a sensible, well-priced sandwich that makes the most sense from an economic, nutrition, and taste standpoint. But if that's not what Silent Steve wants, you won't make the sale. Same thing if you see an inference question on the GMAT... it doesn't matter what you think is logical, you need to read what Silent Steve wants.

"So you need to figure out what he means when he points to his knee. Let's say through trial and error that he wants a meatball sub. Now, every time he comes in and points to his knee, he wants a meatball sub. It doesn't make logical sense, but consumers are irrational."

Discerning an inference question from a reading comprehension passage isn't a matter of black-and-white deduction. The extremely logical aspiring business-school student needs constant reminders to abandon logic and go with the pattern the test maker has established. To hammer this home, every time a student responds to an inference question by getting too logical, I say:

"Silent Steve wants a meatball sub!"

It's an absurd juxtaposition, and through repetition it sinks into their mind that inference questions aren't about optimally rational analysis.

3. *During a freak thunderstorm, a 50-minute middle-school social-studies class has become convinced that a series of weird noises coming from the walls means the classroom is haunted.*

No. We only have 50 minutes to crank out a history lecture. We can't be doing one of the longest joke types to set up and deliver. We've got to snap them back into focus immediately, either with a quick joke ("Those aren't ghosts, they're just students I trapped in there for NOT PAYING ATTENTION TO MY SOCIAL STUDIES LECTURE.") or through another method ("The next student to talk about this or look at the wall loses five points!").

This revisits an important rule: we don't need to be making a joke at every single opportunity. Many great teachers don't even need to make jokes at all. What we all need to be doing is picking and choosing our spots and joke types so we hit on most of the jokes we make. Sure, we can often turn things around and increase retention when our joke gets groans instead of laughter ("Yeah, that one's a lot funnier when you're my dad. Turn to page 45..."). But if just making jokes were the key to retention, there wouldn't be a problem with education; everyone would just flail around making stupid quips and cranking out championship students faster than the "Tearing-up-Furniture Science" department at Cat College.

That's why the key to this whole thing is picking your spots, learning the tested methods, and figuring out which jokes best suit your personality and mannerisms.

Those of you skilled at deduction may also have noted that I said a 50-minute class is not enough time to make a repetition joke. Does that mean you should never make a repetition joke if you are one of the high percentage of teachers who have short class periods? Of course not—that would deprive you of a solid tool and, more importantly, deprive me of book sales. Just keep your eye on the time.

4. *A bunch of corporate trainees taking a day-long business ethics course are preoccupied with planning their postclass golf outing.*

Yes. You've got the time, you've got a distracted class.

I'm not immune. I've been to these "corporate education" retreats where none of us in the audience want anything more than to get out of there/hit the links. One of my favorite training sessions during a corporate retreat was conducted by a 40-year expert who had clearly done her research on how to engage current generations.

We're not all trying to just get to the fun; that's not why we don't want to pay attention. The crowd killer for these corporate retreats happens when we are presented with several hours' worth of information, much of which is either not applicable to every participant or can be found on the internet. What's the point of memorizing all that information when only a fraction really needs to be retained?

This experienced older instructor would start each section with a brief intro, then summarize key information. Then she would pause and say, "Show of hands: how many people find this applicable on a weekly basis?" If less than half of the class raised their hands, she would say, "Alright, when this does come up, here's how you find it on the internet."

Each time we started a new area of training, we were alert. The less interested we were in the material, the more alert we were because we wanted to be sure to vote no when the session leader asked if it was relevant to us on a weekly basis. It was an amazing reversal of the biggest obstacle to retention: lack of interest in the material. Sometimes the instructor would outline an area, pause, then—instead of asking, "How many people does this apply to on a weekly basis?"—would say, "Even if this doesn't apply on a weekly basis, you need to listen." Then she would explain why it couldn't simply be searched for: either the information wasn't out there or there was a wealth of bad info floating around the internet or it would take too long to Google in an emergency, etc. I was so appreciative of the devotion to tailoring the lesson to my specific needs, I'm proud to say that I actually retained some of this information—unlike pretty much every other corporately mandated training seminar I've ever attended.

5. *A substitute elementary-school music teacher is having trouble getting the choir to harmonize on high C.*

Yes. Like most public-school students, I was forced to endure the Geneva-Convention-violating audio torture known as elementary-school band. Our 30-student classroom ensemble consisted of 10 trombone players, 5 trumpeters, and 15 recorder players. Now, trombone and trumpet groups barely sound good when they're playing for a stadium of drunk people who are Pavlovian-trained to cheer for the band that plays every time the home team scores. Getting them to sound remotely unlike an elephant with a digestive system full of brussels sprouts was beyond the skills of my elementary-school music teacher, who I assumed had to take the job as part of some sort of jail-deferring community service.

Also keep this in mind: the brass section was the "good" part of the musical group. The trombone and trumpet, instruments specifically designed to sound like a broken water heater and tea kettle, respectively, were nowhere near as bad as the recorders. The recorders were veritable dog whistles, warning aspiring youth music teachers to stay far, far away. Fifteen of these shrieking whistles proved too much for the ears of my teacher. So he took the 10 worst recorder players and decided to make them into a choir. In the fourth grade, there is only one type of singer: crackling, off-key, and squeaky.

So my instructor came up with the actually genius idea of constructing songs around them holding just one note. Whenever the class descended from a roaring din of cacophony into a sound that proves there is a bright side to being tone deaf, the instructor would have everyone quiet, then point to the choir. This was their cue to try to hit that same note.

The first time, they giggled embarrassingly before making a group screech that sounded like a highway full of suddenly braking cars.

The second time, we all giggled before they made a group screech that sounded like a thousand metal rakes scraping a chalkboard.

The third time... everybody started taking it seriously. The screech had become a silly, pleasant reminder that we all needed to stay on key. Slowly they got better. Not good, obviously, but not punishingly bad. Slowly we got better, the stoppage and note screeching became a funny form of aversion therapy. It was amazing. He was punishing us for messing up, but the punishment was easy to take and didn't single anyone out.

A subtle side benefit, or I guess a main benefit from a teaching perspective, had to do with control. Before the choir, we had felt aimless when we all fell off key. We had to stop and then all start over to make sure we were on the same page. The constant starting and stopping became tortuous, and resetting took longer and longer. By having the choir emit a hilarious burst of "singing" every time we messed up, it brought us a measure of relief and a transition point to ease us back to the beginning. It also made the instructor seem a lot more powerful; instead of trying to herd 30 students back to the start of a measure, he would stop a section, prompt another section, stop them before the windows shattered, start the first section, etc. It made him seem much more like a conductor and less like a tortured prisoner.

6. *On the first day of clown college, a lecture on the history of oversized bow ties keeps getting derailed by a rowdy class of students who won't stop honking their red noses.*

No. The clown college students are clearly interested in their roles and just need to be quickly redirected back to the lecture at hand.

Also, did you get the job as clown-school professor (probably though nepotism), then realize that you weren't funny enough, so you bought this book? Or did you read half of this book and get instilled with such amazing confidence that you went out and signed up to teach clown school? Either way, I'm sorry for my role in your life decisions.

7. *A double-period high-school English class is distracted after a student has an epileptic seizure and is taken to the hospital.*

No. Hey, the two elements needed are there—a long enough time period and a distracted class. However, what kind of joke are you going to make that is in any way appropriate? A tragic situation is never a good lead-in for a joke in an organized class setting.

8. *A half-day kindergarten class is in tears after a student spread rumors at recess that they would all get to watch a popular animated movie starring a sentient toothbrush who discovers there's a cavity... in his soul.*

No. There are two reasons why I love teaching small children. The first is that I have twin hyperactive boys, and I have developed a nasty case of Stockholm Syndrome. Years of my life have been spent metaphorically lashed to a tree while a tornado made of fists and poop blew through my property. The second, slightly more pleasant reason is that their distractibility is both an asset and an obstacle, and it happens constantly. It should come as no surprise to anyone who has ever dealt with children that an entire crying classroom is not as disastrous as your painfully pulsating eardrums may indicate. Forming a joke is more work than necessary—just find the next distraction and watch the tear ducts dry up like a slug in Salt Lake City.

9. *A freak windstorm has knocked out the power to your seventh-grade pre-algebra class, and students are restless because they aren't allowed to leave until the lights come back on or their parents pick them up.*

Yes. You have what is a nightmare for tweens and a dream for repetition-themed jokemakers. You have time to kill.

One of my closest friends likes to teach middle-school classes as a substitute because he likes the challenge—and also because he probably secretly hates himself. Once a windstorm did knock out the power during a lesson on exponents. His go-to for emergencies like this is to play a game similar to *Jeopardy*. He writes categories and dollar amounts on the board, and students team up to answer questions.

However, on this particular day, he decided to try to work exponents into the game in a very subtle way. In real *Jeopardy*, there are only one or two Daily Double spaces, which afford the finder the chance to win up to double their money. However, my friend had a twist. To start, he began each team with $1,000.

The first team chose a question. Only about half the class was interested in the game; the other half was still too excited about the scary-weird development. Suddenly, my friend emitted a high-pitched, warbling wail, which got everyone's attention. He then announced that the team had discovered a Daily Double. They bet all their money because, why not? Then they either won double their money or lost all their money; it doesn't matter which because it's exciting either way.

My teacher friend then had the second team choose a category. He again let out a two-toned shriek that got everyone's attention. They had also selected a Daily Double.

When the third question was chosen, everyone was waiting for it. Sure enough, my friend yelled out the now-familiar scream. It was another Daily Double. The class laughed; they were as involved as a class could get, considering the situation.

Soon the class figured it out: every question was a chance to double their money. It only took a few more rounds for people to see that their money could get astronomical if they answered a streak of questions correctly. It only took them one more round to realize that if they bet all their money every time, they would eventually miss a question and go back to $0.

At this point, my friend paired everyone off and asked them to come up with a strategy to ensure they would end up with the most money while not risking all of their money each time. His plan worked. The humorous repetition of the Daily Double warble had been entertaining and attention-grabbing. Each pair then presented their strategy, with my friend translating it to algebraic equations.

10. *Your four-hour LSAT prep class hasn't gotten a question right in 20 minutes. Even basic, obvious ones. They are tired.*

Yes. I'll show you how to deliver this during the actual lecture without risking a time sink. But first I want to point out that while I was teaching this particular LSAT class, I had a bladder infection that caused me to have to use the restroom every half hour. Rather than panic about having to leave an already distracted class seven times each session, I said...

"I can work with that."

Every time I'd have to leave for the bathroom, I'd give the students a practice problem to keep them busy. Upon returning, I'd often find that students had finished the problem early and spaced out, or didn't even fully attempt the problem. So each time I returned, I would fling the door wide open and shout:

"[Student Name], what did you get for step one of the method?"

Next time I came in, I'd fling open the door:

"[Different Student Name], what did you get for step one of the method?"

Pattern established, I could play with it a bit:

[Fling door open] "[Different Student Name], what did you get for step one of the method? Also, what did you get for step two?"

Soon enough, every time I flung open that door, everyone's heads would snap up. They thought I could call their name at any time. Really, I had it planned out where I would start with the most inattentive students. That way they'd pay attention to at least getting through step one. Turns out, it put the whole class on high alert because the ones who weren't called on enjoyed giggling at whomever I had chosen to scrutinize. I wasn't expecting miracles, I just wanted to get the most sluggish students motivated to get through at least one step. I mean, come on, I had a tired class and a bladder infection. Did you expect me to move mountains in there?

So even for busy classes, there is usually an opportunity to use out-of-class time to set up a repetition that eventually translates to humor. I'm not even sure how it works, something about the human mind being trained to put things into patterns. After all, the thing humans are better at than any other animal (besides pouring beer so it has the perfect amount of head) is arranging the zillions of atoms in a room into a cohesive picture. For most animals, eyesight is limited to recognizing predators/prey/food that's about to fall off a table. So perhaps it's extra jarring when the human mind gets a pattern interrupted. Why does it cause laughter? I don't know, I'm just spitballing evolutionary science here. The point is it works and it's easy.

But for school teachers, the rapid pacing of transitions in and out of class really leaves minimal room for repetition setups outside of class time. Luckily there's a good way to do them in class should the need arise. It's a method that's been used by almost every sitcom since the beginning of time: create and repeat a catch phrase.

Sitcom writers have leaned on catch phrases like they lean on having dysfunctional home lives. It's because the repetition of the catch phrase creates laughter without the writers actually having to spend time or effort creating a situationally relevant joke. So how do we translate this technique to the classroom and increase retention? Make a catch phrase that summarizes a key concept of your lesson, which is underscored several times throughout the class period.

Teaching history to middle schoolers can be a chore. Some of them are not old enough to recognize the value of learning history, but not naïve enough to just sit and pay attention for 50 minutes. So when I had to teach history to sixth to eighth graders, I'd make sure to summarize my points at various times throughout the lesson, always with the same phrase. Usually that phrase is a variation of "Because these people didn't learn from the past. Probably should have paid attention in history class."

The area of history that is the most difficult for me to get middle schoolers interested in (without humor) is financial cycles. So I turn to humor. Or, rather, I turn to repetition, which somehow creates laughter through a process that may or may not involve comedy.

Here it is in action from real lessons I taught to some preteens in an after-school program. If you thought middle schoolers were checked out during school, imagine how little they want to pay attention to after-class lessons.

Say I needed to talk about economic bubbles. There's nothing that is more boring to tweens than Dutch people buying tulips 500 years ago. So when I finish that part of the lesson, I ask, "So why did everything turn out horrible?" Then I pause, as usually someone shouts out something funny that gets the class energized. Then I add my catch phrase, "Because the people involved didn't pay enough attention in history class! Economic bubbles always burst."

Then I talk about the roaring '20s and the stock market crash of 1929. Nobody in my class cares, so I have to bring it around by detailing how their own families could wake up and suddenly find themselves destitute. Then, the catch phrase: "So why did everything turn out horrible? Because the people involved didn't pay enough attention in history. Economic bubbles always burst."

Once I have established the pattern through repetition, it can be weaved into the back-and-forth of the class. If I call on Claire and it's clear she wasn't paying attention, I can rib, "Claire wasn't paying enough attention in history class. Apparently, Claire loves the Great Depression." Or: "Steve wasn't paying enough attention in history class. Maybe I should just quit my job and sell tulips to Steve all day!"

Not pictured: The sour stench of economic collapse

QUESTION

One of my favorite things to teach about standardized tests is that, for the reading comprehension, details rarely matter. If a question does concern a minor factoid in the passage, the test taker can always look it up. This is true for the SAT, GRE, LSAT, and many other standardized-test passages.

However, as excited as students get to learn that they don't have to pay attention to boring details in science or history passages, it's easier to talk about than execute. Our brains want to pay attention to details when we read—that's what most reading is about. So getting students to gloss over details often involves painful repetition of mistakes. Did somebody say repetition? Yes, I did, because I set this whole thing up and also I am the only one talking.

What's the best way to humorously hammer home the concept that details don't matter?

A. Make everyone repeat the mantra "Details don't matter, details don't matter, details don't matter" after reviewing each passage.

B. During paragraph-by-paragraph guided practice, ask a question about a detail for each paragraph. No matter what the answer is, reply, "Details don't matter."

C. Instruct students to write "Details don't matter" next to every paragraph when they are taking the actual exam.

D. Every time a student accurately remembers a detail, make them write "Details don't matter" on the board.

E. Going over a passage, stop after every sentence and ask, "Is this a detail? Is it important?"

Answer: **B.** *During paragraph-by-paragraph guided practice, ask a question about a detail for each paragraph. No matter what the answer is, reply "Details don't matter."*

Reading without taking in details is difficult. Students need to rewire their brains. So after every paragraph, I remind them and hope they will read the next paragraph for only the structure and tone, not the details. It provides just enough repetition with a four- to six-paragraph passage so that students get some laughs out of it and the message sinks in.

WRONG ANSWERS

A. *Make everyone repeat the mantra "Details don't matter, details don't matter, details don't matter" after reviewing each passage.*

Just like with my annual New Year's resolution to get in fewer fistfights, saying it doesn't make it happen. Plus, making a class repeat a cult-like chant after they've read an entire passage is not the best idea. It's like telling someone to duck after they get punched by an angry comedy teacher.

C. *Instruct students to write "Details don't matter" next to every paragraph when they are taking the actual exam.*

This would waste a lot of time, and standardized exams are always timed. Also, if they're taking the exam, the window of opportunity for me to teach them anything has closed.

D. *Every time a student accurately remembers a detail, make them write "Details don't matter" on the board.*

This is mean. I especially can't imagine doing this with an adult student.

E. *Going over a passage, stop after every sentence and ask, "Is this a detail? Is it important?"*

This is too frequent. By the 10th time or so, everyone will hate you. It also wastes too much time demonstrating only one principle.

I wanted to bring this example up for a reason. There are other times you can use repetition for retention besides when a class is tired or distracted. Just make sure to work it in naturally so it doesn't cut into time that should be spent teaching, and don't repeat it too often (once every few minutes is usually good).

Formula 6: Personification
Target Audience: 3- to 12-Year-Olds
Warm/Cold Audience: Warm

I was substituting for a fifth-grade social-studies class. I don't know if their regular teacher was lax or if they had had too much turnover to establish a routine, but this class was wild. It took me five minutes of class time just to settle them down. The last thing I wanted was to make a joke and risk losing control again.

Then it happened. As I was detailing the results of the American Revolution, something that American students should actually be interested in if nothing else, a paper ball hit me square on the chin. I looked up in time to catch the culprit. The class, fortunately, was quiet.

I said to the class, "What if I sent Chris to the office, but he refused to go?"

A question that apparently appealed to the rebellious class, as they remained listening.

"How could I make him leave? Could I make him leave? This was the exact same scenario the British faced when they wanted to regain control over America."

I stepped over to Chris's desk and said, "This is purely hypothetical, I would never do this for real...but what if I tried to pick him up and carry him to the office? Chris, what would you do?"

"I would punch you," Chris said. He was straight to the point—I can respect that.

"Okay, say Chris punched me and also, probably, kicked me really hard." Laughter. I don't recommend slapstick as a teaching tool, but as a hypothetical visual aid it's alright.

I asked, "Who won the fight?"

The class thought for a moment before someone volunteered, "Chris won. He didn't go to the office."

"That's right!" I declared, then proceeded to explain how difficult it was to make someone leave or gain control of them if they resisted, and that was why the underdog American forces were able to repel the British and form their own country.

Class went better after that. It wasn't Stand and Deliver *exceptional, but the class was engaged by the exciting visual and humorous hypothetical.*

By personifying the two sides of the American Revolution, I created a relatable (and intense) metaphor that the class could follow. It helps that I was talking about a battle. If I were lecturing about the westward expansion of American settlements, I might've had a harder time working the conflict into a metaphor. ("Pretend Chris is a settler and that paper ball was barbed wire. Also, I am a cow.")

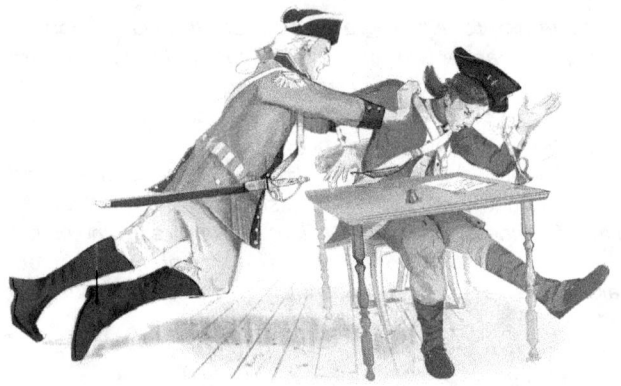

In a way, the fledgling United States was like that unruly child. In a way, it kinda still is.

Naturally, this works well with students acting out because they clearly want attention. The other area where impersonation and personification work is with young students. Personification is a great way to engage and entertain. *Sesame Street* has alphabetic letters singing songs and doing dances. The other day, my five-year-old son came in, wearing my glasses and shoes, and declared, "Look at me, I'm a big, dumb guy." Personification is funny. While you may not think that last example is educational, believe me, I learned the slow burn that comes from being the subject of good insult comedy.

Now I'm not talking about dressing up like a historical figure for an entire lesson. That only engages a class on television, and wigs are hot and itchy. You might be saying, "Hey, I had great success dressing up like an apple for my lesson on gravity." Okay, fine, go with it. But it never engaged me—I was too cool to enjoy a good impersonation, like most dumb teenagers.

QUESTION

During a second-grade PE class, a student named Dweezil won't stop swinging his jacket around. How could you best use personification to let it sink in that this is unacceptable?

A. "Dweezil, if you aren't more careful, you could hit someone with your jacket, and then you might hurt it!"

B. "Look at me, I'm Dweezil. My dad was Frank Zappa, so now I get to act like a dangerous idiot!"

C. "I'm the gym. It makes me cry when I see Dweezil swinging around a jacket!"

D. "PE is your god, and you are displeasing him!"

E. "If your jacket was a person, you'd be bonking its head on everything and causing severe chronic traumatic encephalopathy."

Answer: **A.** *"Dweezil, if you aren't more careful, you could hit someone with your jacket, and then you might hurt it!"*

This is a great way to warn someone when they are purposefully ignoring stern reproaches. Plus, you can't always be sure that Dweezil has enough empathy to understand that other students can be hurt. It may sound weird, but a lot of kids are little sociopaths until around 10 years old. But every kid cares about his stuff. Making him care a little more can be the key. Also, I've used this joke in this exact situation half a dozen times, and it always gets results. So stop questioning my methods, geez!

WRONG ANSWERS

B. *"Look at me, I'm Dweezil. My dad was Frank Zappa, so now I get to act like a dangerous idiot!"*

Ignoring the fact that Dweezil Zappa hasn't been in second grade for over 40 years, this is pretty mean. Personification doesn't mean mockery.

C. *"I'm the gym. It makes me cry when I see Dweezil swinging around a jacket!"*

The logic just isn't there. If concern for fellow students isn't going to make Dweezil stop, then concern for a gym character certainly won't either.

D. *"PE is your god, and you are displeasing him!"*

This is scary. Plus there's not a person alive who believes that PE is a god, not even PE teachers (for most of my PE teachers, oddly enough, square dancing was their god).

E. *"If your jacket was a person, you'd be bonking its head on everything and causing severe chronic traumatic encephalopathy."*

Personifies the right object, but ends on a confusing and extremely farcical scenario. Anyone with kids knows you don't threaten with impossibilities (unless that impossibility is the punch line, such as the jacket getting hurt in choice A).

Formula 7: The Grand Opening
Age Group: All
Cold/Warm Audience: Cold

I'll never forget the first time I met my all-time favorite teacher. It was the first day of junior year in high school, and I was in US history. We had heard a lot about the teacher, Mrs. G. She was regarded as one of the best orators in the school and was in charge of the honors history courses.

When I first entered her classroom, I barely noticed her. Her five-foot-two frame was swallowed up by an enormous desk, twice as wide as the desks of most teachers. Stacks of papers covered the desk, some as high as her head when she was sitting down. I remember thinking, "How can she have stacks and stacks of papers already? It's literally the first day of school. Are these left over from last year? Is this teacher any good?"

Though my grades were high, I had a lot of issues with school. I had frequent outbursts, which were frequently unfunny and unwanted (unlike today, where my interruptions are frequently funny and unwanted). The teachers who were angered or overwhelmed by my boisterous, and frankly obnoxious, nature were not teachers I ever made a connection with. I liked direct teachers, assertive teachers, teachers who could take my callouts, censure me, then turn it into a teaching moment.

I saw none of those characteristics in my initial assessment of Mrs. G. She wasn't even looking up at any of her new students. Disappointed,

I slumped into the nearest available chair and awaited a year of learning boring history facts from an underwhelming speaker.

But then the bell rang and her perfect delivery began. She stood up, meekly, and surveyed the room.

"So, so I guess..." she stammered, "I guess you all kind of like where you've chosen to sit? No one has any need to sit anywhere else?"

The class shook their heads and murmured nos. They were already getting distracted.

"Wellllll, TOO BAD!" Mrs. G shouted, as our backs shot upright with alarm, "Because I have a seating chart! James Adams, where are you? Sit over there! Christine Baduk, where are you? You're sitting over there!" Everyone else, here's the seating chart on my desk. You have one minute to get to your new seat or I'm docking you five points!"

My opinion of her had flipped faster than a steak whose juices have stopped being pink. Here was someone bossy, extremely assertive, and best of all...pretty freaking funny.

My year was amazing. I had no problem staying engaged and even managed to improve my self-monitoring enough to significantly reduce blurting out quips without being called on. I didn't want to step on her tempo or mess up some bit she might be doing. To this day, I know way more facts about US history than I will ever have any practical use for.

Mrs. G went on to become principal and then, I think, queen of the school district or something. Her demonstrating the unmatchable power of a solid opening joke shaped how I teach and how I plan out all of my comedic ventures—like my lesson plans or my stand-up routines or my parenting.

There are teachers who want to assert authority by being strict and domineering. Another school of thought is that personable, relatable teachers have the easiest job controlling a class. I say why not have both? A great opening joke can be a key part of that.

In fact, paving the way to assert and maintain control over your class is one of the two main purposes of a solid first-day-of-class joke. The other is to showcase your best teaching qualities to earn respect.

Let's examine how Mrs. G used her opening to gain control over the class: she shouted at them and bossed them around. It's as simple as that, yet there's an elegance to it. If a humorless teacher opens the first day of class by shouting and brusquely ordering me to sit somewhere else, I'm going to wonder why the teacher is being mean and perhaps a little mentally unhinged. I'm definitely never raising my hand out of fear of the weird, angry teacher erupting. But Mrs. G's class didn't have that problem—people regularly volunteered contributions to lessons and discussions. Why?

To understand this, we must deconstruct the methods, delivery, and structure of her opening bit. So buckle in and grab a coffee because this is going to require a lot of unpacking. Here we go.

She used a 180-degree-turn joke.

That's it. We're done unpacking. Sorry for setting you up there; I've just always wanted to make a 180 joke where the punch line is "It's a 180 joke."

I didn't give the 180 joke its own section with instructions and activities. This is because the 180 is covered sufficiently in the Grand Opening and 1-2-3 sections. Think of it as a 1-2-3 joke without the 1 part. Just start a statement in one direction, then take a sharp turn at the end. "Every morning there are students pounding on my classroom door…demanding to be let out!"

You may have noted that, although the opening joke is for the beginning of your lesson, this joke is detailed last in this book. It's because the Grand Opening joke isn't a separate type of joke; it should use one of the formulae already outlined. In this case, she used a 180. This achieved two purposes:

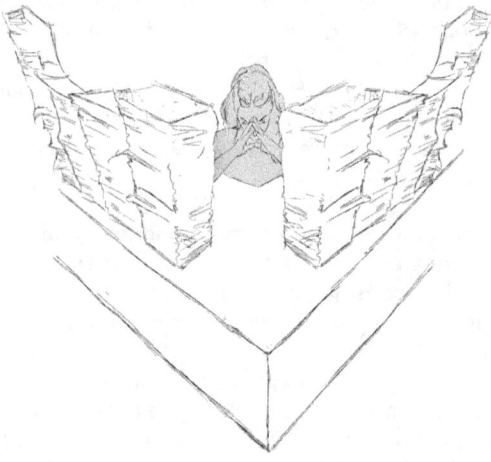

My wife used to have the same issue with giant stacks of papers. Then she bought a huge book on organization, which gave her another surface on which to stack papers.

First, she showed that despite being a hard-driving task manager, she had a great sense of humor. There's a common perception that many teachers are just humorless, unfeeling sticklers. I know at least half of my teachers came off like people who were strict at school and then went home and lectured to their wrinkled suit until it stiffened out. That's not relatable to a kid or a teenager. Actually, that's not true as a blanket statement. Being super rigid is unrelatable to 99 percent of kids and teenagers. There are always those one to two people who like dry classroom patter and have perfect attendance and never do anything fun and eventually become president of the United States (because our presidents always have spotless records in their youth). But for most students in most classes, that caricature of the utterly inflexible stalwart of schooling is shockingly true. I like teachers who are experts at their subject and know what they're doing, but I don't like teachers who are experts due to an inability to perceive anything that isn't a bland fact related to their particular subject.

The other purpose achieved by a solid opening joke is to set the tone for how you will run the class. To craft this, you'll need to know what classroom skills you are best at. In Mrs. G's case, it was keeping the class moving efficiently, assigning tasks rapidly, and having a powerful personality. Her opening showed two things: she made the students move in order to show her powerful personality, and she got everyone seated within a minute, putting her devotion to efficiency on display.

QUESTION

Though your public-speaking persona can be underwhelming, you have carved out a great career, thanks to your ability to notice all sides of an issue. You can spot points that your students may not have considered. In short, you are strong at playing devil's advocate in order to encourage students to think laterally. Which of the following jokes would be best as an opening to showcase your talents and preview how you expect the class to go?

A. "I see too many students wearing hats, even though my strict no-hats-in-class policy is punishable by hellfire!"

B. "There are three things you need to know in order to succeed in this class: One, always wear your safety goggles when you are at your lab station. Two, do not handle any chemicals unless you are wearing safety gloves. Three, follow the other dozen safety protocols written on the wall! These are dangerous experiments and safety isn't effortless."

C. "We are going to have a great time this year, provided that none of your smiling faces gets MELTED OFF BECAUSE YOU'RE NOT FOLLOWING SAFETY RULES!"

D. "James has a green backpack. John has a pink backpack. Does that mean you two are going to fight?"

E. "Don't clean the beakers so well you can see your faces in them. They might break because you are all ugly."

Answer: **B.** *"There are three things you need to know in order to succeed in this class: One, always wear your safety goggles when you are at your lab station. Two, do not handle any chemicals unless you are wearing safety gloves. Three, follow the other dozen safety protocols written on the wall! These are dangerous experiments and safety isn't effortless."*

Devil's advocate! You act like everything is covered, but there's a whole bunch of other things students probably never considered. This is a great opening joke that showcases your skills and kickstarts your students' retention of safety rules.

WRONG ANSWERS

A. *"I see too many students wearing hats, even though my strict no-hats-in-class policy is punishable by hellfire!"*

Enough with the hats already! This might be an okay exaggeration joke but you don't want to open with it. Hats don't matter, and it makes you seem a bit too eager to get people to laugh at everything.

C. *"We are going to have a great time this year, provided that none of your smiling faces gets MELTED OFF BECAUSE YOU'RE NOT FOLLOWING SAFETY RULES!"*

This 180 is alright, but it doesn't really showcase what you do best: explore and show that there are always more angles to be explored. This is why you are in charge of safety. You are a stickler for every rule. Let them know that right away with your opening. Putting the fear in them is great, but it's not as complete as B.

D. *"James has a green backpack. John has a pink backpack. Does that mean you two are going to fight?"*

Whoa, now! Too aggressive!

E. *"Don't clean the beakers so well you can see your faces in them. They might break because you are all ugly."*

Okay, this one is obviously too mean to make a good opening. But that's not why I included it. The key mistake is that you're encouraging them not to do something that they actually should be doing. They should be cleaning the beakers thoroughly. If you can't make a joke that follows the correct class procedures, just don't make a joke. Every single class every single year doesn't need a dynamite opening. Relax a bit.

To further dissect the concept of designing your Grand Opening joke to highlight your style, let's examine my opening joke for this very book: The one where I melt down because Plato never said anything nice about comedy. It was designed to showcase my best aspects and help me maintain control. Now, the part about maintaining control may seem silly at first. After all, it's my book; I'm the only voice. There will be no callouts or dissent from the readers, so how could I possibly lose control?

If that's what you were thinking, then you vastly overestimated my ability to not screw things up.

To research this book, I read a horse-cart full of articles and short books on how to be funny and how to teach. I was, to say the least, disappointed by most of them. There were too many gimmicks that relied on being wild and goofy and not enough formulae and situational comedy help. These gimmicks, generally known as "monkey-cheesing," will be covered in chapter 3, but for now let's focus on how I crafted my opening joke.

Naturally, the way to increase your odds of immediately endearing yourself to readers is to lead with your best foot. So when crafting my opening joke for this book, I began by making a list of my best qualities:

- Painful self-introspection. If I'm doing something that's not funny, I can't ignore it or blame it on my audience. It's always my fault. Naturally, that places an exhausting amount of pressure on me. That's what I do, and the people in my life benefit from it, so just get in the caravan and leave the stressful driving to me. I like going over every single aspect of a class or a conversation or an argument to perceive things from not only my point of view but also to speculate on how the other people involved perceived me. Then I come up with a plan to do even better next time. Then I utterly fail to execute that plan properly and chalk it up as good practice.

- The ability to turn bad times into great moments. When it comes to the classroom, I can walk into a horse stable and emerge with a huge, steaming lump of gold. It has gotten to the point that whenever something goes poorly in my classroom, I get excited because it's another opportunity to turn real-world strife into a teaching moment.

- Public speaking. When I was a child, I was hyperactive and had a speech impediment. When I fixed my speech impediment and got the hyperactivity under control years later, all I wanted to do was explain things to as large an audience as I could muster. As such, standing in front of people and speaking—one of the most common fears among people—is oddly cathartic for me.

I've stood in front of 50 people at a comedy club and bombed for five straight minutes. I've never been so relaxed. Of course, later, I went home and painfully examined every single second of my act. Because public speaking has such a serene effect on my demeanor, it's easy for me to figure out how to fix a bad situation in the moment. I can use my talent of turning childhood trauma into good comedic teaching tips so you can get there in a matter of hours. Which leads into my final best quality:

- I love making people happy. It's my favorite hobby, figuring out what a group or an individual really wants, then determining the best ways to give it to them. Whoever coined the phrase "You can't please everyone" has never been to one of my parties.

Those of you who enjoy reading the titles of books probably noticed two glaring omissions from this list of best qualities: teaching and comedy. Well, now that we're deep into this tome and I probably already have your money, I can share with you the big secret that had me paranoid about how to start this book…

I'm not particularly exceptional at teaching or comedy. At least not enough to deserve to write a book about it.

Sure, I'm good at teaching. I've done it full time for almost a decade and part time for decades before that. My student reviews are almost always positive. But that just makes me a solid teacher; it doesn't make me amazing enough to write a book. If you earned a degree in teaching, I'm sure you probably know twice as much theory as I do. If you've taught for 20-plus years, I'm sure you probably know dozens more great teaching tips than I do.

Yes, I'm good at comedy, enough to build a full-time writing career that spanned decades. But that doesn't make me good enough to write a book on comedy that would be able to compete for shelf space among all the tomes penned by famous A-list comedians. I'm just good enough to make a salary, nothing more. Even that isn't all my doing—I owe it to my wife's willingness to relocate to Los Angeles. I have a lot of friends who have way more talent than I do but who had way less career success than I did. The only difference between them and me is that my wife was willing to uproot everything and relocate to where the business takes place. My all-time favorite 180 joke I've ever written is, "My wife is perfect in every way except one…horrible taste in men."

What I am good enough to write a book about is…and those of you who made the mistake of reading the title before you opened this book have the spoiler as to how this sentence is going to end…using comedy to teach. I know the joke-writing formulas, I know how to use them in the moment to refocus a class and, most importantly, I know when not to use comedy (which is, frankly, most of the time).

So when I sat down to outline this book and figure out my opening, I knew I wanted to showcase my best qualities and apply them to teaching with comedy. However, I wanted to do this *without* actually saying something that's related to just teaching or just comedy. Because if I open a book with a statement that I've learned about teaching, everyone with degrees and more experience is going to roll their eyes and either think it's wrong or remedial. Same with comedy.

Needless to say, this had me pretty nervous. In fact, it took me a whole month of prep before I could write word one of this book.

But it wasn't that I was blocked, it was more like there was a mountain in my path I had to climb. How do I sell myself as an expert in teaching with comedy without purporting to be an expert in teaching or comedy? How do I work my Grand Opening joke around my strengths to hide my many, many, *many* weaknesses?

I decided to open with a history. If you want to convince most teachers that something is important, you show how it has shaped the history of teaching. Simple enough, I thought. I sat down and researched the history of teaching with comedy, expecting a light-hearted-but-effective jaunt from ancient comedic educators to the present.

Those of you who chose the optimal strategy of reading this book from the beginning know that this plan worked out horribly. Turns out no one used (or at least recorded) anything about teaching with comedy for the first 1,000-plus years of literacy.

So I was super frustrated.

That is, until I realized that this matches my list of qualities quite well.

For example, I wanted to demonstrate that I can turn bad moments into teaching points. So I should talk about failing at finding relevant history. I wanted to show I can introspect with the best of them. Admit disappointment, right there on the first page.

Note how, because I had my list of qualities I wanted to illustrate, the joke practically wrote itself. All I had to do was place readers in the situation I encountered. That's situational comedy, the best kind.

 I hope you realize the parallel between my outlining this book and your creating a lesson plan. If not, then do.

Let's revisit my Grand Opening joke. It took a few pages, so I'm just going to present an abridged version here:

"Using comedy to increase student retention has a long and storied history. It dates back perhaps to the first teachers ever. And who is the most famous ancient teacher? Plato, of course. Check out what this zany educator had to say about combining teaching and comedy:

> *For ordinarily when one abandons himself to violent laughter, his condition provokes a violent reaction. If anyone represents men of worth as overpowered by laughter we must not accept it, much less if gods.*

Well, okay. It looks like Plato hated comedy. Not what I expected, but I can work with that. For instance, how many of Plato's teachings can you actually recall? I can't think of any, in part because he was from a long line of humorless instructors with dry, deadpan delivery."

Mess up, get disappointed, admit it, then turn it around to show I can make jokes and roll with the punches. Also, dunk on Plato—that always scores points.

QUESTION

What do the following two things have in common?

1. **My Grand Opening joke about Plato unexpectedly contradicting my argument**
2. **Mrs. G's opening joke where she seemed meek, then shouted, "Too bad!" and began bossing the class around**

A. They are both 180s.
B. They both cement us as authorities that shouldn't be questioned.
C. They showcase our deliberate, carefully scripted mannerisms.
D. They would work for students of any age.
E. I ripped both jokes off from the television show *I Love Lucy*.

Answer: **A.** *They are both 180s.*

Both jokes start with a setup (Mrs. G is meek and overwhelmed; I have carefully researched jokes by Plato to support my claims), then take them in a totally different direction (Mrs. G cracks a joke and then powerfully orchestrates the class; I list three quotes by Plato that don't support my initial claim).

Does every Grand Opening joke have to be a 180? No. It's just that showing off your best qualities fits so well into the 180 format because doing what you do best is so effective. Leading off with the opposite behavior, then BLAM! switching right into your most powerful methods is going to jar people into laughter. Or at least, into paying attention and paying you a bit of respect.

A 180 turned out to be the best tool to showcase both of our styles. What joke type is best for your Grand Opening? Well, that's what this whole section is about.

I chose each wrong answer to highlight an important point.

WRONG ANSWERS

B. *They both cement us as authorities that shouldn't be questioned.*

First of all, they obviously don't cement us as authorities. My joke was specifically designed to highlight that I can roll with things when I am wrong. Mrs. G's joke was designed to show that she can take control. It's not like she's trying to show that she's an authority of implementing seating charts.

Even more than these specifics, I (and all of the teachers I surveyed) don't want to sell themselves as the end-all expert on the test material. No matter what the age group, it's not effective. With kids under 10, they already think all adults are the authority on everything, and also built the school and are old enough to show vacation slides from the Civil War. With tweens and teens, leading with a strict attitude that I should never be questioned makes many of them *want* to question me. These students love to push limits. I loved to push limits when I was their age. You might be thinking that it's a bit paranoid to base my teaching styles almost exclusively on how I acted as a student when I was at my worst. To this I say, "Okay. Maybe. I don't have to be perfect. Are you done attacking me? Good, let's get back to the material."

The teaching job I worked the hardest for, the teaching job I love most, is teaching advanced standardized tests for graduate-school admissions. Stuff like the GMAT for business students, the LSAT for aspiring lawyers, and the GRE for those who want to start a career but would like to rack up tens of thousands of dollars of student loan debt first.

Sure, teaching adults is the area in which I see the most improvement for my efforts. But even more than that, I like teaching these graduate standardized tests because the students are, without exception, universally neurotic.

This statement may surprise you, to which I say two things: One, have you actually been to grad school? It's bursting with nuts like a squirrel's cheek. And two, "neurotic" isn't meant derogatorily. These students are all so driven that they are willing to spend a fortune on higher education and give up their evenings for several weeks to take my class to better their scores on a single test.

So there's a lot of pressure and a lot of stress: The GRE classes have a lot of people getting their teaching degree who suffer from math anxiety. The GMAT classes have extremely focused future business managers who realize how competitive their fields will be. The LSAT classes have future lawyers, a highly competitive and high-pressure profession.

Every graduate class I get has these anxious people who are depending on me to bring up their test scores. Do I want to open the class by assuring them that I am an expert at everything?

Hold on, let me phrase this as a question so you can feel engaged. It's getting near the end of the book and I don't want to lose you.

QUESTION
For standardized-test classes with adults, do I want to immediately establish myself as an expert who has full mastery of the material?

A. No.
B. Yes.
C. Sure, why not?
D. Totally.
E. Definitely.

The answer is **A.**

The thing about standardized tests, and the reason why I score 95th percentile or better on each and every one of them, is because they are not designed to test someone's knowledge. You think I get 95th percentile on the LSAT because I have an encyclopedic knowledge of everything related to the field of law? Of course not—that would be a ridiculous underuse of such a skill. More importantly, it would be something I can't teach to students in just a few weeks (first night's homework: read and memorize everything about law).

The reason why I do so well on these tests, and the reason why my students eventually learn to do well also, is that they are designed primarily to test common-sense wits. Take the question above... if you hadn't even read the question, you could get the answer merely by looking at the choices. There's only one right answer, so since four of the answers are functionally identical, you know they must be wrong.

That's how these tests work, believe it or not. College admissions boards already have a good picture of the body of information a student has amassed and how they performed in a classroom setting; that's what grade point average measures. What colleges want from these standardized tests is to see who can think on their feet and who can get the answer in the fastest way. (As with the question above, the fastest way is usually not "solve the problem using your no-doubt complete body of knowledge.") In fact, I would often go as far as to say that standardized tests frequently want to punish the people who have an encyclopedic knowledge of the material because those people aren't efficient and are super weird to work with.

So with my openings to my graduate standardized-test courses, whether I use a joke or not, I want to sell that I am *not* an authority on the subject. I'm just a normal guy who can keep his wits about him when confronted with a problem he has no idea how to solve.

Honestly, with any standardized exam, about one-fourth of the questions completely baffle me upon first glance.

That's what students need to hear to get fully motivated. I get high scores even though I'm not an expert, and so can they.

In fact, establishing oneself as an expert can often have an opposite effect: it can demotivate certain students. "Math anxiety" is a common term for students who have given up on themselves when it comes to learning math. To them, it's either a skill you are born with or you aren't, and they weren't. Sadly, this affects women more often than men,[20] and many women are told by school instructors that they "just don't get it."

So when I step before a group of graduate students, many of whom probably have math anxiety, I definitely don't want to come off like "I'm a man who understands all math, that's why I score high on the GRE." That reinforces the whole "you get it or you don't" adage.

Moreover, the GRE in particular loves to prey upon this weakness by giving questions that seem impossible but actually involve very basic math. The following is one of my favorite problems to open a GRE course with. Math-anxiety students have a lifetime reinforcing their opinion that "you get it or you don't," yet this problem frequently flips their opinion to "yes, I can do it" in under a minute:

☾$n = n + 2$

☾$2 = ??$

The symbol varies: sometimes they'll use that crescent moon, sometimes they'll use a clover, or a heart, or whatever children's cereal marshmallow they happen to prefer. Why is it that they can use interchangeable symbols?

Because the symbol itself has no actual mathematical basis. It's not math. No one looks at this and says, "Oh, hmm yes, crescent moon math, I know this."

Why do they do this? Because they're not trying to reward people who know math. A lot of GRE test takers plan to major in some sort of theory-intensive field. That means they'll regularly be tasked with reading hundreds of pages dissecting a simple concept, probably written by someone who does not have English as a primary language. Colleges want to know who can look at that confusing body of text and extract the basic principles being outlined, and who will just give up.

That's the purpose of the crescent moon question—to present something that every single person will find unfamiliar and see who can spot the basic principle at work.

What is the basic principle at work? Well, if ☾$n = n + 2$, then ☾$2 = 2 + 2$. You just substitute the number next to the moon for n.

It's like if your grocery list says ☾n = buy n, then ☾cornflakes = buy cornflakes. Except instead of "buy" in the math problem, ☾ means "add two to whatever is after the ☾."

They are literally asking, "What is 2 + 2?" The students who give up because they don't "remember" what moon means (which, interestingly, includes both the students who are really underconfident in math and those so overconfident that they don't apply common sense to confusing questions) will miss it. All the students who hang in there and consider the problem will realize that it's just asking, "What is 2 + 2?"

However, we should always be asking ourselves if a joke is even necessary. As it turns out, there is a far simpler solution than creating and practicing a deliberate opening mistake.

That solution? Just don't make a deliberate mistake and play the first hour of class straight.

Why does this work? Okay, cards on the table here. During every hour of every class, I am almost definitely going to make a mistake somewhere without deliberately trying. I don't ace these standardized tests because I'm perfect; I ace them because I stay calm and don't panic.

So GRE class starts, I don't make an opening joke. Eventually, I make a mistake, and either I catch it or (much more likely) a student catches it. Great! We're all set up for a punch line that can show students how to catch mistakes themselves and alleviate math anxiety. Something like, "Wow, I made a mistake there. Let's say I proceeded to solve the problem, got an answer, then saw that my answer was not one of the choices. Do I panic and scream, then utterly give up/start punching people? No. Well, sometimes. But usually, I assume I made a simple mistake because I know my weaknesses and oftentimes it's simple arithmetic. Then I go back and check my work…ah, there's the mistake. I correct it, and now I have the right answer!"

See how that works?

1. Identify your strengths.
2. Guide your opening to emphasize those strengths.
3. If it helps, make a Grand Opening joke.

One of my strengths is keeping composed when making a mistake, so I've practiced a way to make that a strong positive and allow for some humor. The humor is almost not necessary, which is why I don't script it ahead of time. However, it does make a person remember the fact that "composure while making mistakes is just as valuable as actual knowledge on the GRE."

Now, let's go over the other three wrong answers. Remember them? I promise I won't spend five pages on each one!

C. *They showcase our deliberate, carefully scripted mannerisms.*

No, the whole point is that we use comedy in the moment to make an impression, increase retention, and steer things on track. If you're a rigid teacher with everything planned, that's cool: you do the best you can. But the point of this book is to show how to generate comedy specifically by celebrating the unexpected/undesired.

D. *They would work for students of any age,*

You probably don't want to shout, even facetiously, at a bunch of sensitive toddlers. Also, bossing people around can rub adult students the wrong way. It's important to cater to your target audience. If only there was a chapter on that…

E. *I ripped both jokes off from the television show* I Love Lucy.

Well, this is obviously a throwaway joke to round out the question. Let's move on.

Oh, wait, earlier I wrote, "I chose each wrong answer to highlight an important point." Hmmm…

Okay, I'm going to level with you, here, dear readers. Writing a book takes a long time, between writing this book and the editing process, I've spent over a year on it. I first wrote up this question nine months ago. By the time I had finished my lengthy spiel on wrong answer B, I forgot to explain the other wrong answers.

We just noticed this omission, and I'm trying to fix it. I'm sitting here in my office, which is what I call whichever room my computer is currently in (right now, it's my kitchen). I'm sitting here wondering what amazing point, what no-doubt groundbreaking piece of teaching advice I meant to show with the line, "I ripped both jokes off from the television show *I Love Lucy*." Nine-months-younger me was so much wiser. Let's just say "Don't rip off jokes, that falls under the `reference comedy' category of mistakes" and move on.

Let's examine some other common teacher characteristics and discuss which joke structures would best highlight their strengths on the first day of class. Let's do it with some workbook questions:

QUESTION

It is the first day of teaching a high-school calculus class. In fact, it is the first day of your teaching career. You know the material backward and forward, having honed your skills in your Eastern European country, where you were head of aerospace engineering for the

military. Unfortunately, another thing you honed in your lifetime in the Eastern Bloc is a thick accent. What's the best Grand Opening joke?

A. "An old Eastern European joke: What is shaped like a potato and has dozens of eyes? A potato. Also the back of my head, so PAY ATTENTION!"

B. "I was head of aerospace engineering in my home country, so I know my stuff. However, you might find me difficult to understand, and the reason for this is obvious: you are intimidated by my awesome math skills! Don't worry, you'll get over it."

C. "English-speaking students have a lot more trouble understanding me than my students in my home country. No doubt the reason for this is clear: you are stupid at math."

D. "If my words sound funny to you, rest assured it's because I'm drunk."

E. "There are three things you need to know in order to take my class: One, I am an expert at math; two, I have a thick accent, so I will often repeat myself; and three, I am an expert at math."

Answer: **E.** *"There are three things you need to know in order to take my class: One, I am an expert at math; two, I have a thick accent, so I will often repeat myself; and three, I am an expert at math."*

This is a tightly constructed 1-2-3 Grand Opening that hits on everything you want to say without a lot of excess setup: you are great at math, and you have a thick accent, but you are aware of it and have a sense of humor about it. There aren't any excessively big words which students could mishear, and the repetition punch line means that students don't need to understand every word you say to get that you are making a joke about your thick accent.

WRONG ANSWERS

A. *"An old Eastern European joke: What is shaped like a potato and has dozens of eyes? A potato. Also the back of my head, so PAY ATTENTION!"*

This highlights that you have a thick accent, which is your weakness, yet doesn't bring up your sharp knowledge of your subject. That's not the goal—you want to highlight your strengths, not just lay out your weakness. Also, the potato joke has nothing to do with your strengths or weaknesses. When a good portion of your Grand Opening joke is filler, it's a good sign you probably want to drop the joke entirely.

B. *"I was head of aerospace engineering in my home country, so I know my stuff. However, you might find me difficult to understand, and the reason for this is obvious: you are intimidated by my awesome math skills! Don't worry, you'll get over it."*

This answer is good: you lay out your strength and weakness right from the start. However, it has some flaws that aren't present in answer choice E. First of all, it contains a bunch of big words. If clarity is your weak spot, don't increase the difficulty of your joke delivery by mixing in a bunch of multisyllabic, complicated words. Also, and we haven't touched on this just yet, which is why I included this wrong answer, *sarcasm is extremely difficult to use on the first day.* Understanding when someone is being sarcastic requires experience with their speech patterns and attitude. If you open your class with the joke from answer B, there's a reasonable chance a lot of students won't pick up on your facetiousness and will simply assume you have a huge, condescending ego and don't realize how thick your accent is. Don't risk it—save the sarcasm for after students get to know you.

C. *"English-speaking students have a lot more trouble understanding me than my students in my home country. No doubt the reason for this is clear: you are stupid at math."*

So this one is obviously wrong, but what exactly is wrong with it? First, you never mention that you are really great at the subject matter. That's the whole point of the Grand Opening: to highlight your strengths. Teachers who find themselves focusing too much on humorously explaining away their weaknesses should ask themselves if they could benefit from being a bit more positive. Rest assured, no matter what your weaknesses are, students will totally notice them and resent you for them. So be confident!

Also, don't call your students stupid. Even if they know you well enough to interpret it as sarcasm, it's not positive, which can lead to an overall classroom air of negativity, which hurts retention. If you want, you can say, "If you don't understand me, is this because you are stupid? Of course not. I have a thick accent." It's still not the most effective Grand Opening because it doesn't promote your strengths, but it's better than outright calling your audience stupid. If you didn't catch this, you're stupid. (See what I did there? It's going to revolutionize the dad-joke industry.)

D. *"If my words sound funny to you, rest assured it's because I'm drunk."*

This one won't work, obviously. I didn't include it as a tempting trap answer, but rather to emphasize that you shouldn't outright insult yourself, frankly, ever. There are a lot of easy ways to show awareness of your shortcomings without highlighting them. The way we're illustrating here is to couch them around a humorous summary of your strengths. Also, the drunk part is a lie. I want to be very clear on that, dear reader.

Let's examine a situation that's almost the polar opposite of the one described above.

QUESTION

You are called in to substitute teach a high-school algebra class. Upon arriving with your well-drilled lesson plan and worksheets, you realize that there was a mistake. You are actually teaching French 2. No problem—well maybe one small problem: you don't speak a word of French. However, one of your strengths is that you have an imposing physical presence and a deep, booming voice. What Grand Opening will best facilitate the class participating fully even if they aren't confident in your mastery of the subject?

A. "I'm going to have you all do most of the talking for the class today. This is because I am confident that your regular teacher has instilled the skills in you to further your own growth without a lot of babysitting. This is not because I don't know French... yes... they don't suspect a thing..."

B. "Open your books to wherever you left off last class, and don't ask any questions unless they are in English because this is America!"

C. "I'm not going to lie to you. I thought this was algebra class. So just bear with me if I make any huge mistakes... unless they are algebra mistakes in which case you can tear into me."

D. "You're not in your old teacher's world anymore. You're in my world, and my world is an abattoir. There, that's a French word!"

E. "Repetition is key! When you answer, you will answer in French, then say it in English, then in French again! Got it? WRONG! The correct answer is 'Oui, yes, oui!'"

Answer: **E.** *"Repetition is key! When you answer, you will answer in French, then say it in English, then in French again! Got it? WRONG! The correct answer is 'Oui, yes, oui!'"*

You've highlighted your strength: lots of exclamations give you many chances to showcase your imposing presence in a constructive way, and you will use it to get the exact responses. You also created an instant-translation rule, so you won't ever feel clueless as to what the students are saying. Also, it was a short statement, always a plus.

WRONG ANSWERS

A. *"I'm going to have you all do most of the talking for the class today. This is because I am confident that your regular teacher has instilled the skills in you to further your own growth without a lot of babysitting. This is not because I don't know French... yes... they don't suspect a thing..."*

Cute, but you don't want to do a whole bit where you credit their old teacher, then unravel, then talk to yourself. That's trying too hard.

B. *"Open your books to wherever you left off last class, and don't ask any questions unless they are in English because this is America!"*

Come on, now. This is French class; they should speak a lot of French. Not only is this bad pedagogy, it's not very subtle. Students are going to figure out you don't know French because you were so insistent on speaking English. It's like when one of my sons runs downstairs and declares, "Don't look in the upstairs closet!" I can guarantee that the upstairs closet contains a terrified house cat dressed up as a dinosaur.

C. *"I'm not going to lie to you: I thought this was algebra class. So just bear with me if I make any huge mistakes...unless they are algebra mistakes, in which case you can tear into me."*

There's a difference between being honest about your shortcomings and openly declaring you are unprepared for a class. Even with young students, you want to keep focused on providing quality service: some of these students actually want to learn, so declaring you aren't prepared can slam the door on their motivation to pay attention.

God sometimes runs down the stairs and tells me, "Don't look upstairs!" That's how I know it's going to rain.

D. *"You're not in your old teacher's world anymore. You're in my world, and my world is an abattoir. There, that's a French word!"*

Your goal is to assert authority without them realizing you don't know French. So threatening them with a French word is like doubling down on your gamble. Also, abattoirs are bloody. You don't want that blood to paint your students' first impression of you.

Let's do one more.

QUESTION

Your strengths as a sixth-grade science teacher are numerous and strong. You are great at breaking down complicated processes into simple steps and encouraging students to push through each part. You are a great coach. However, your style requires participation. It requires people to be willing to work and to understand. An unruly student or lots of callouts can really derail you.

What is a solid Grand Opening joke for your style?

A. "If you talk out of turn, I will send you immediately to the office. Now let's have some fun breaking down complicated science concepts, which I am really good at."

B. "Take a look at this skeleton. That's going to be you if you interrupt my awesome breakdown of science with a callout."

C. "I see some of you did not bring your science books. Those of you who did bring your science books, I must ask you … did you steal their science books?"

D. "I'm really good at explaining the tough stuff that might have confused you in previous years, but in order to help me help you understand it, you must do three things: One, keep your eyes on me when I am talking; two, keep your mouth closed unless you raise your hand and are called on; and three, don't use the lab equipment to make chemical warfare weapons that violate the Geneva Convention."

E. "I like to explain things and answer questions without interruption. So if this entire class goes by and nobody speaks out of turn, you all get five extra-credit points … and if you do speak out of turn, I can't protect you from the wrath of all 30 of your classmates. Well, I could, but I won't."

Answer **E.** *"I like to explain things and answer questions without interruption. So if this entire class goes by and nobody speaks out of turn, you all get five extra-credit points … and if you do speak out of turn, I can't protect you from the wrath of all 30 of your classmates. Well, I could, but I won't."*

This is a nice exaggeration joke: it explains why you need students to focus, it creates a reward/punishment system to make students also take interruptions seriously, and it uses a joke to assure that students retain the information that don't talk equals bonus, talk equals everyone gets mad at you.

WRONG ANSWERS

A. *"If you talk out of turn, I will send you immediately to the office. Now let's have some fun breaking down complicated science concepts, which I am really good at."*

Veteran teachers know that you can't let the office handle your discipline. The overworked administrators are going to get sick of that quickly and start emptying mousetraps into your school mailbox. Plus, a 180 where the reversal is less emphatic than the setup is a really difficult delivery. While comedy masters like Bob Newhart have made a career out of this style, it's not something a teacher needs to try. It's much more likely that students are too fixated on the "one strike and you go to the office" policy to pay attention to anything you say afterwards. Watch out for that with 180s. Make sure the second part (the punch line) has at least as much oomph as the first part (the setup).

B. *"Take a look at this skeleton. That's going to be you if you interrupt my awesome breakdown of science with a callout."*

Call me a progressive, but I think it might be a tad too much to threaten to skin a student and remove all their organs just for calling out. This kind of extreme facetiousness on an exaggeration joke usually backfires: students know you won't actually go through with your threat (what would you possibly do with all those organs?), so the whole statement lacks punch. It's similar to when frustrated parents threaten a huge punishment, like lobbying congress to outlaw Minecraft. The kids know that you won't follow through on a wild punishment. Even if you are into extremely sadistic punishments, what parent has the energy to go through with it? The empty threat does nothing to deter the bad behavior.

C. *"I see some of you did not bring your science books. Those of you who did bring your science books, I must ask you…did you steal their science books?"*

You may have noticed that none of the Grand Opening jokes I have demonstrated are of the schlemiel-schlimazel type. Teasing/blaming students right from the start usually comes off as mean-spirited. After all, the students haven't gotten to know you. For all they know, every class will start with you making a wild accusation. Due to the nature of repetition, this will probably get hilariously funny about the fourth or fifth time you do it, but by then the whole class will probably be of the collective opinion that you are an unhinged jerk.

There also hasn't been a Grand Opening demonstrated here that uses the repetition joke type. That takes too long; you don't want to take too much time in the beginning. Just show the class what you're about and get right into the lesson plan.

D. *"I'm really good at explaining the tough stuff that might have confused you in previous years, but in order to help me help you understand it, you must do three things: One, keep your eyes on me when I am talking; two, keep your mouth closed unless you raise your hand and are called on; and three, don't use the lab equipment to make chemical warfare weapons that violate the Geneva Convention."*

First of all, always monitor your 1-2-3 jokes, whether as opening jokes or not, to make sure they're not rambling too long. Jokes are quick tools to get a class back on track, not lengthy bits designed to fill up spare time. That's the first thing that's wrong with this joke—it's too long. Also the punch line is too far out and silly. "Don't use lab equipment to make nuclear weapons" is way shorter and conveys the same meaning. It's still not a good joke, but it's quicker. The main reason why this joke will fail to increase retention is because the punch line is distracting. You tell that to five-year-old me, and all I will be able to think about all day is whether I could really make a serious weapon in class. This has no effect on me remembering that I need to keep my mouth closed and eyes focused. A good punch line should enhance the setup with situational relevance, not distract from the purpose of the whole statement.

Speaking of distraction, let's go over the jokemaking traps that can derail the well-crafted jokes you can now create.

CHAPTER 3
COMMON JOKEMAKING TRAPS

Making a joke is like navigating a field of buttery crayons... there are so many ways you can slip up. Yes, my kids are bad at picking up toys and washing their hands, why do you ask? If you're one of the many people who think they have a good sense of humor, but rarely get a laugh, you probably are simply falling into one of the following joke-delivery traps.

Jokemaking Trap 1: Telegraphing

Telegraphing is revealing that a punch line is coming. Even if a joke is delivered with good timing, it can still fail to get a laugh and thereby hurt retention if one gets too excited during delivery.

The whole essence of joke telling is that you establish a rhythm and a logic with the setup. Then, the punch line upends that logic while maintaining the rhythm so that people notice the slight change a moment before they recognize that it's offbeat. The comparison between the normal rhythm and ridiculous logic creates a disconnect in their minds, which leads to laughter... hopefully.

It's easy to get excited and lose the punch line. Some people do it because they mistakenly think every punch line should be delivered with a vaudevillian amount of pomp and circumstance. In the vaudeville era, there wasn't nonstop comedic media available, so audiences weren't as keyed into the flow of a joke, and performers needed to announce their punch line had arrived. We don't need to do that anymore; the average student today has consumed far more joke-telling media than even the most experienced vaudeville actor. All a joke needs is a little difference in rhythm or cadence and people will know the punch line has arrived.

I don't even like it when someone tells me,
"Hey, I have a joke for you," because then I know
the punch line is coming. Yeah, I'm super fun at parties.

QUESTION

Which of the following jokes does *not* dangerously oversell the setup?

A. "Every hero has a fear: Indiana Jones was afraid of snakes, Ron Weasley hated spiders, and while I didn't actually see this film, I assume the lead character of *Moonlight* was afraid of werewolves."

B. "I'm a big fan of punishing students. For instance, yesterday there were some students obnoxiously knocking on my door. Finally I couldn't take it anymore, so I got up and let them out."

C. "It hasn't been the best week with my visiting exchange student. In fact, I just dropped her off at the airport. Her flight is two days from now."

D. "My grandparents have been happily married for two years. They just celebrated their 50th wedding anniversary."

E. "I've been through a lot. I've lost friends in the war, I've lost lovers… most of whom were the girlfriends of the friends I lost in the war."

Answer **D.** *"My grandparents have been happily married for two years. They just celebrated their 50th wedding anniversary."*

It's a short 180, it's tight, and it opens with a weird statement that should get students' attention—*not many people have grandparents that just got married two years ago*. Then it's resolved quickly (you've already got people's attention, now get out quick and get back to your lesson). You probably want to pause a bit after the punch line in order for people to try and solve your math riddle (I am a sucker for a situational joke where the punch line is a number).

The main purpose of these carefully selected and precisely botched jokes is that, as teachers, we often lean toward overexplaining. Great for educating students about complex concepts, but horrible for getting students back on track with a quick joke. Let's unpack the other answer choices.

WRONG ANSWERS

A. *"Every hero has a fear: Indiana Jones was afraid of snakes, Ron Weasley hated spiders, and while I didn't actually see this film, I assume the lead character of* Moonlight *was afraid of werewolves."*

Almost a tight 1-2-3, it just botches the dismount. First line establishes the pattern that heroes have fears. It's quick, it's not a radical idea, and it puts the audience right into pattern-expectation mode. The first two items quickly express the pattern: hero and fear. The third one conflates a coming-of-age drama with a B-list horror movie theme. However, what's the punch line? The punch line is that you haven't actually seen the movie. Stick your punch lines at the end. Watch how that improves the joke tenfold:

"Every hero has a fear: Indiana Jones was afraid of snakes, Ron Weasley hated spiders, and the lead character of Moonlight *was afraid of werewolves."*

Now, students who are familiar with *Moonlight* will pay attention because it had nothing to do with werewolves. It's time to resolve the discrepancy with the real punch line:

"I assume. I actually didn't see the movie."

This punch line includes some explanation and it also interrupts the list pattern. That should be enough to catch your audience's attention. Then we hammer home the pattern failure by admitting we didn't see the movie. The point is we get attention by misunderstanding a famous movie and disrupting a pattern. Eyes now on you, you can segue back into your lesson.

B. *"I'm a big fan of punishing students. For instance, yesterday there were some students obnoxiously knocking on my door. Finally, I couldn't take it anymore, so I got up and let them out."*

A classic template joke that I've repurposed for a classroom setting. So what sent this joke into treacherous-delivery territory? First of all, the punch line is telegraphed with the opening line, "I'm a big fan of punishing students." The 180 is supposed to go in a completely opposite direction, not change the course of the joke back to the original direction.

Also, note that overexplaining it pushes it further into dad-joke territory. Instead of a tight 180, it's now a joke where two-thirds of it is explaining how mean you are. Note how the first sentence adds nothing while detracting from the punch line. Students will know you're strict when you reveal that you imprison other students in your classroom.

Think about movie antagonists. How do we know they are super bad? It's never because they declare, "I am super bad!" That's not engaging. Instead, great villains show us their depravity with their actions. In fact, growing up, my friends and I had a rule that if ever anyone states something about themselves, tune it out. It's either part of some weird joke or anecdote, or it's wish fulfillment on their part. If their self-reflection is so true, then it should show in their actions and not have to be stated.

C. *"It hasn't been the best week with my visiting exchange student. In fact, I just dropped her off at the airport. Her flight is two days from now."*

Again, don't make blanket statements summarizing what you are about to say. It's great for educating and incredible for writing expository essays, but not conducive to bringing students back to focus.

One of the things we are going for here is a sort of trickle effect when it comes to laughter. A few students will get it at first, then their laughs will make other students pay attention to find out, "What's the joke?" Even if they don't quite get it, they are actively engaging with what we are saying.

There's an easier way to remember this without all this theory and practice. Just keep your 180s going in one direction until the last line. So instead of "It hasn't been the best week with my visiting exchange student," reverse it and say:

"It's been a great week with my exchange student. I just dropped her off at the airport. Her flight is in two days."

There we go, a nice 180 that should get a few students laughing and most of them wondering, "What's the joke?" Also, as I mentioned before, it's way easier to transition out of a failed joke if it's understated. If nobody laughs, you can quickly transition back into the lesson so the result shifts from "failed joke" to "peppery banter."

E. *"I've been through a lot. I've lost friends in the war, I've lost lovers... most of whom were the girlfriends of the friends I lost in the war."*

This one gets kind of rambly, is hard to decipher, and isn't appropriate for a classroom setting. But that's not what we're here to learn. We're here to learn about telegraphing punch lines. This punch line is that the joke teller was shacking up with their friends' girlfriends while the friends were off at war.

Another extremely common reason people "overdeliver" the punch line is that they get too excited about the accolades they will receive in the form of audience laughter. Nothing turns an audience off more than someone who smiles and shouts out their punch line like it's the most brilliant thing ever discovered. I once broke up with a long-term girlfriend because she would deliver every joke with a smug look on her face and a lilted voice pregnant with the expectation of a laugh. No, really, that was the reason. Well, that and the fact that she insisted I was too petty.

That was a joke: I complain about some minor thing my ex did, and then complain she thinks I'm petty (which I am because I complain about minor things my ex did). Let's examine that last joke as if it were delivered orally. Changing the tone during the punch line utterly undermines the point of the punch line, which is that I am totally unaware of my own shortcomings. The punch line must be delivered straight, in the same manner as the setup, because the fact that I'm unaware that the punch line *is* a punch line is the entire essence of the joke.

Again, there's that great reason to work on your delivery: to make sure you're not overselling the punch line. It's far more difficult to recover from a boldly delivered punch line that doesn't get a laugh than a failed joke with an understated punch line.

QUESTION

Let's say you practice and practice but still can't deliver a muted punch line. That happens a lot because telling a joke is tough. Which one of these jokes WON'T be ruined if you change your tone leading up to the punch line?

A. "There are three things I love to teach to people: one, geometry; two, grammar; three, how to stay awake while learning geometry and grammar."

B. "My family did a traditional Thanksgiving. We commemorated the relationship between settlers and Native Americans by fighting ALL THE TIME!"

C. "Who wants to demonstrate this problem? Uh oh, check out Rajesh. He's not looking up at me. That means hellfire! Rajesh, come demonstrate this problem."

D. "Remember, repetition is the key to remembering that the formula for combinations is n factorial divided by r factorial times n minus r factorial. Repetition is the key to remembering that the formula for combinations is n factorial divided by r factorial times n minus r factorial. Repetition is the key to remembering that the formula for combinations is n factorial divided by r factorial times n minus r factorial. Repetition is the key to remembering … stuff."

E. "Rachel has a blue pen. Robert has a black pen. Is this like a rival gang colors thing? Are you going to fight?"

Answer: **C.** *"Who wants to demonstrate this problem? Uh oh, check out Rajesh. He's not looking up at me. That means hellfire! Rajesh, come demonstrate this problem."*

When you are still mastering keeping an even delivery, exaggeration jokes are your go-to formula. Changing your cadence/volume/pitch can actually help your exaggeration joke. It lets students know that you're not really serious. So when you say something like, "Not making eye contact means hellfire," with a smile on your face, students don't need a good delivery to know you are joking. Not only that, the exaggeration should be delivered in a different vocal way than the setup. After all, it's an exaggeration, not a muted punch line. If you're still learning the ways of delivery, consider practicing some exaggeration jokes.

WRONG ANSWERS

A. *"There are three things I love to teach to people: one, geometry; two, grammar; three, how to stay awake while learning geometry and grammar."*

Here's why telegraphing the punch line with your mannerisms will undercut this joke. First of all, let's examine the purpose of this quip. Obviously, it's to increase retention, as geometry and grammar tend not to be the most popular subjects. You don't want students to go into the lesson expecting a slog of boring lists and facts. Making the first list you present end in a 1-2-3 joke will hopefully encourage them to think that if they pay attention, there might be some reward besides a brain ache.

Note that our goal is to get our students interested, not to get you a laugh. If you quickly and evenly deliver this joke, regardless of whether people laugh, you'll have established that your lessons will be broken up with some entertaining parts for those who are paying attention. If you deliver the punch line with bravado, then pause for laughter, one of two things happens. Either they don't laugh, and probably dread the grammar and geometry lessons even more knowing that more bad jokes are coming, or they do laugh, and you've established only the exact same amount of increased retention as if you had delivered the joke evenly. It's an easy risk/reward analysis. Don't oversell your punch lines.

B. *"My family did a traditional Thanksgiving. We commemorated the relationship between settlers and Native Americans by fighting ALL THE TIME!"*

So what happens if we change our inflection delivering the punch line? First, it makes it sound like we are telling a joke. Your goal of increasing retention through 180s is to work these jokes in as natural conversation. Sure, there's a great market for sounding like you're telling a joke—it's called stand-up comedy. In the classroom, we just want to increase the class's attention and get back to the lesson.

Second, this is a situational joke. It's funny because a lot of families fight at the Thanksgiving table. My mom once left a calm Thanksgiving with her mother, father, and four siblings to use the bathroom. When she came back minutes later, no one was there. They had gotten into an argument and all stormed off.

That's the true purpose of this joke. Presumably, it's being delivered after the four-day Thanksgiving break, and we want to get students back into school mode. A funny reminder that, after a long weekend with family, some kids may run back to school.

Third...what, you're going to deliver a punch line about your family fighting all the time and the plight of Native Americans while smiling? That's kind of psychopathic. No offense.

D. *"Remember: Repetition is the key to remembering that the formula for combinations is n factorial divided by r factorial times n minus r factorial. Repetition is the key to remembering that the formula for combinations is n factorial divided by r factorial times n minus r factorial. Repetition is the key to remembering that the formula for combinations is n factorial divided by r factorial times n minus r factorial. Repetition is the key to remembering...stuff."*

Repetition is the key to remembering stuff, especially if that repetition is done the same way with each iteration. Also, you never know exactly where the laugh is coming in a repetition joke, or if it is coming at all. It would stink to carve out time for such a long delivery and then botch it by getting excited and messing up the tempo before you get to the payoff. Repetition jokes are high-risk, high-reward. Out of all the formulas in this book, I'd save mastering repetition for last.

E. *"Rachel has a blue pen. Robert has a black pen. Is this like a rival gang colors thing? Are you going to fight?"*

With schlemiel-schlimazel, the goal is to ratchet up the tension. Tension between students is a draw for the entire class. Playing this joke anything but straight is going to dissolve the tension. Plus, you can count on at least most of the class not assuming you are serious, so there's no need to be lighthearted with your delivery.

Jokemaking Trap 2: Reference Comedy

Using reference comedy is the most common mistake made, not just by teachers but by anyone trying to add humor to a situation.

Reference comedy is calling attention to the similarities between something that is said/happens in class and a piece of popular media. For instance, during the summer of 2017, one couldn't mention pickles online without someone blurting out, "I'm Pickle Rick!" referencing a plot from the popular show *Rick and Morty*.

I can see why so many people lean on reference comedy. They want to hit their target audience, so they pick a piece of pop culture that their audience likes and they mention it. What could be wrong with that?

Well, there's only one thing wrong with that … and it's that there are exactly three things wrong with that:

1. It takes the class farther away from the subject at hand. The whole point of humor in the classroom is to increase retention of the subject and steer a distracted class back to the subject matter. Referencing some unrelated piece of pop culture does the opposite; it adds even more distraction to the situation.

2. It requires paying attention to media your class enjoys. Every teacher will most likely have at least one show or movie or whatever students consume in common with their class. The problem is, every time you want to make a reference, you have to go back to that limited pool of common media. That gets stale really fast.

3. It's not funny. It's not even a joke. It's just stating, "Hey remember that joke from that thing? That certainly was popular and shared a word or two with whatever unrelated thing we are currently discussing."

Again, this is the most common trap I see teachers falling into. It can feel safe if the joke was good on its original run so you're sure to get a laugh or two. But it's not engaging or organic. If you're wondering whether what you do falls under the odious blanket of reference comedy, it's simple to figure out. Ask yourself: do you reference some element of popular culture? This includes impersonations, catch phrases, and references to characters or plots. It doesn't even have to be current. References to old stuff, such as TV shows and weird news stories, are even more likely to come out of the oven stale. Here, the oven is your mouth.

The good news is that you don't have to lean on the horribly ineffective device of pop culture references. That's why you bought this book, isn't it? You're one of the good ones, and it will show in an uptick in focus and retention from your class.

Jokemaking Trap 3: Taking Too Long

I met my wife in 2006, and she means the world to me. She is a great mother, a wonderful wife, and a partner at a national law firm. In fact, she's perfect in every way except one: she has horrible taste in men.

We're not here to tell jokes. We're here to teach students using the most effective pedagogy tools possible. A joke should only be a quick adjustment to get a derailed class back on track. If the joke itself derails the class, then, obviously, it's doing the opposite of its intended purpose.

Taking too long to tell a joke always derails it.

Take the joke about my wife. I don't need to say all those words to indicate I love my wife. She's my wife, that's all I need to say for people to naturally assume I love her. By listing all those good qualities, I run the risk that my audience is going to tune out because *they already assumed all those things*. Well, maybe they didn't assume she's a partner at a law firm, but that's because they've never seen her stare a man down in court until he breaks into tears. I could simply say:

My wife's perfect in every way except one: horrible taste in men.

Save the long-winded joke for your hour-long comedy special. In class, we need to be quick so we can get right back to teaching. If the joke has more than two sentences, it had better be an integral part of some lesson activity, like the example about the coal-mining town and how it applies to median and mode.

I came up with the joke about my wife in response to repeated queries from my classes on how to ace the law-school standardized test. Since hearing of my wife's success making partner at a national law firm, my students bombard me with questions about how she did it (years of hard work), where she works (a law firm), what her LSAT exam scores were (medium), and a whole bunch of other things that I love to brag about but *have absolutely nothing to do with anything on the actual LSAT.*

So I wrote a quick joke. It's only one sentence, 12 words. It deflects attention from the students' endless questions, and even if they don't laugh, they pause to appreciate what I'm saying, which allows me to smoothly transition back into the scripted lecture without having to cut someone off.

QUESTION

Here is a multisentence joke that goes on too long. All of the sections can be cut but one. Which one?

Crazy people have the ridiculous notion that being good at math corresponds with being good at the GRE math section. In fact, you can actively hate math, have a picture of math up on your dartboard, and post angry rants on math's Facebook page but still do great at GRE math with some simple practice. Now, I don't hate math because when I was a kid, math was my only friend. I devoured equations like Cookie Monster devours blood pressure medication. But still, at least half the time when I look at a GRE math problem, I am initially baffled. Is that because I just don't get math? No, it's because the test is designed to stymie even the most math-fluent nerds... er, I mean totally well-adjusted people.

A. "Crazy people have the ridiculous notion that being good at math corresponds to being good at the GRE math section."

B. "In fact, you can actively hate math, have a picture of math up on your dartboard, and post angry rants on math's Facebook page but still do great at GRE math with some simple practice."

C. "Now, I don't hate math because when I was a kid, math was my only friend."

D. "I devoured equations like Cookie Monster devours blood pressure medication. But still, at least half the time when I look at a GRE math problem, I am initially baffled."

E. "Is that because I just don't get math? No, it's because the test is designed to stymie even the most math-fluent nerds... er, I mean totally well-adjusted people."

Answer: **B.** *"In fact, you can actively hate math, have a picture of math up on your dartboard, and post angry rants on math's Facebook page but still do great at GRE math with some simple practice."*

When in doubt, always ask yourself, "What's the point of whatever I'm trying to say?" Here, it's that people don't have to be comfortable with math (*at all*) to do well on the GRE. Only the second sentence says that. If the second sentence didn't have a joke, that's fine.

As always, never sacrifice the clarity of your message for a joke. Jokes are like soldiers in the war of educating reluctant students. There is no soldier so superior that you don't wait to sacrifice them if it means winning the war on retention. Also, you can sometimes get as much engagement with a repeated war metaphor as with a tight joke.

WRONG ANSWERS

A. *"Crazy people have the ridiculous notion that being good at math corresponds to being good at the GRE math section."*

This almost gets the point across, except it does the total opposite. We want to hammer home that you can be bad at math and still do well on GRE math sections. Stating that being good at math doesn't necessarily equate to doing well on the math GRE risks that students won't make the connection.

C. *"Now, I don't hate math because when I was a kid, math was my only friend…"*

Just one part of an elaborately set-up joke. It's about me, not about the point I'm trying to make.

D. *"I devoured equations like Cookie Monster devours blood pressure medication. But still, at least half the time when I look at a GRE math problem, I am initially baffled."*

This is the second-place winner. It underscores that the GRE math test is not a typical math quiz. However, it doesn't bring my anecdote around to show why the audience can do great at GRE math problems, which is a flaw. One of these days, I'm going to make that Cookie Monster diabetes bit work in a way that increases retention.

E. *"Is that because I just don't get math? No, it's because the test is designed to stymie even the most math-fluent nerds…er, I mean totally well-adjusted people."*

Again, this touches on the point but doesn't make it directly relatable to the target audience: people who are nervous about doing math.

Long-winded joke telling can be rectified with the advice mentioned in chapter 2—don't write your jokes ahead of time. In the comedy-writing industry, it's called riffing. In the musical-theater industry, it's called "forgetting your lines," but in the comedy-writing industry, it's a good thing, trust me. In the heat of the moment, it leads to way more quick, organic moments for humor.

Riffing can seem terrifying to people who are nervous about their delivery skills, but let me put your fears at ease: I've been writing jokes for decades, and riffing still terrifies me. So what do I do?

The key is my attitude. If I mess up a joke, I'm not embarrassed. I just own it, "Wow, I messed that up. Anyway, back to learning about rhetorical essays." It's not the end of the world.

Landing a joke isn't something that comes naturally to most people. However, the people who are naturally funny almost universally have one key trait in common; they have self-confidence in their ability to deliver humor and don't really care too much if a joke lands or not.

That last part can be tricky to master. You have to not care if everyone laughs at your joke and not care if your joke is met with the silent, icy glares of a million disappointed students (in your slightly overcrowded classroom).

This is crucial, though, for several deep reasons. First, it is instrumental in making sure you don't oversell the punch line. It also shows that you can recover from a bombed joke. Finally, it emphasizes the most important point of all. *It's not about you.* It's not about feeling great because you made the class laugh, and now you'll be thought of as the "fun" teacher, and students will stop spray-painting rude caricatures on your car. It's about getting students back on track when something distracting threatens to derail their learning.

There's a really simple way to get over the fear of bombing a punch line in class: get up on stage at a comedy open-mic night and bomb there.

Call it extremely accelerated immersion therapy. Once you tell a joke to an ovation of utter silence, everything else becomes easier. Don't bring friends because they'll laugh. I used to bring my dad to all of my stand-up shows to avoid the silence that comes after a poorly delivered joke. My dad hates my comedy, too, but he coughs all the time.

Once you've felt that rock-bottom feeling of angry eyes boring into you because you were supposed to make a good joke and utterly, utterly did not make a good joke, it's way easier to take a quick risk in class.

If you still feel nervous even after that, there's an even easier way to avoid bombing: just don't tell jokes in class.

Seriously, being funny isn't a requirement, and if it's not for you, don't force it. You are fully capable of being an amazing teacher without any jokes or refunds for comedy-writing books that did nothing for you.

Jokemaking Trap 4: Puns and Wordplay

Try not to make puns or plays on words. That might be redundant, I don't know, because I've never touched this bread and butter of the dad-joke world. I have several colleagues who swear by using puns to foster student retention. To them, I always say, "Hey, if it works, go with it. However, just so we're clear, you know a groan is not a laugh, right?"

Still, if you're dead set on incorporating puns into your teaching, just be sure that you don't oversell your delivery. I'd rather have a teacher whose words dry out all of my earwax than have one who constantly makes quips based on wordplay like they're telling the world's best joke.

Common Jokemaking Traps

There's a simple and effective way to make sure you won't steer a class off track with your punmanship (or...punWOMANship!).

Do you see what I mean? Overselling the pun just makes it worse.

In order to keep the class moving forward, only make puns that are extremely relevant to the lesson at hand. Here are some dos and don'ts of using puns to increase retention and keep students focused.

Do:

- I don't know what you want from me here, dear reader. I told you to probably stop making puns and yet you're still reading this section. So we've already determined you are dead set on ignoring the things I say. I can work with that. Maybe you'll heed my list of don'ts if I follow them up with really uncomfortable examples...

Don't:

- *Don't* make puns that require an elaborate setup.

There are two things I regret doing in elementary school. First, spending time learning math formulae that required elaborate storytelling mnemonic devices. Second, picking on Plato at recess because he had no friends.

Here's something I learned growing up:

There once was a king of France. He wanted to go around the world teaching geometry. So he walked all the way around the world until he came to a man who didn't know who he was. He said, "Sir, I come from France. My path around the world is its circumference."

This wasn't helpful or optimal for learning a very simple math concept. First of all, how did the king walk across the ocean? Or did he go north to south, making a bizarrely twisting and turning path to stay on land masses? Why did the man he met not recognize him? If he went around the world, he should be back in France, so why doesn't random dude recognize his own king? And why does the king call this disrespectful guy "sir"?

Thoughts like these would always occupy my mind for about 10 minutes after each of these "story mnemonics." I'd finally refocus and realize I'd missed a good chunk of the lesson. I'd also realize that I hated clunky wordplay.

It wasn't until a year after I was first introduced to the concept of circumference that my friend said, "Dude, it's just 'circ' for 'circle' and 'ference' for 'fence.' It's a fence around a circle and you need to know how long it is." There it is: simple, direct, and clear. It stuck with me immediately and forever. The biggest difference between my friend's explanation and the king story? My friend's explanation wasn't a joke. I can't say it enough, so I'm just going to restate it at every opportunity: many times a joke isn't needed, and it actually introduces the unwanted possibility of losing the class.

- *Don't* make puns that say the opposite of what you're trying to teach.

The situation is also implausible because *circumference* is not a French word.

Another outdated mnemonic device they pushed on me as a kid was supposed to help me memorize the formula for the area of a circle. That formula is pi times the radius squared, or πr^2.

"Pi aren't square!" My teacher would quip using an exaggerated southern drawl, "pi are round!"

The class chuckled, but when test day came, I would write "πr^2" on my paper, then cross it out because pi aren't square.

- *Don't* use an established teaching play on words without examining it for ways it could be improved.

In the comedy world, there's a saying: "Puns are lazy." It's very true—puns are the baseline currency of those who don't want to come up with comedy that is situationally relevant. Because of this, even the best, most established puns and plays on words can be scrutinized for ways to improve.

Let's revisit the area of a circle. At some point in time after my childhood, everyone collectively agreed that the phrase "pi aren't square" was a horrible way to teach a simple formula, so they needed a new pun. Really they didn't, which is my whole point, but eventually a new mnemonic was designed using supercomputers or billions of educational funds or maybe just half a pot of coffee in a smoke-filled teacher's lounge. The new, current, preferred methods of teaching the formulae for area of a circle (pi *r* squared) and circumference of a circle (pi times the diameter) are:

Circumference = π x Diameter
Cherry Pies are Delicious. C = π x D
Area = pi x Radius Squared
Apple Pies Are Too. A = P x r^2

Great, they fixed the area formula, but in their lazy rush to attach this to the circumference formula, they made a slip that leaves a lot of room for mistakes. Do you see it? Look at the circumference mnemonic again:

Cherry Pies are Delicious. C = π x D

Now compare it to the area mnemonic. What's different?

Apple Pies Are Too. A = π x r^2

See it? In the area formula, "are" stands for "radius." But in the circumference formula, "are" stands for nothing! This is really, really lazy because anyone could look at the circumference formula for two seconds and say, "Okay, let's change it to Cherry Pie Is Delicious."

The point is, if you insist on using established pedagogical wordplay, give it a once-over for any lazy errors.

Now you might be thinking, "Hey, why all the pun hate? Why don't you show us how to use puns effectively?" The answer, which I feel like I've said before is, "I don't like puns and elaborate wordplay jokes as tools for increasing retention." The key word is *jokes*. "Apple pies are too" isn't a joke, it's just a helpful phrase. With puns and wordplay, you probably won't need to make a joke to increase retention. Keep in mind that jokiness sometimes comes with the strong risk of blurring the message.

QUESTION

You are teaching a cooking class because that is something you do now. Which of these statements would be most effective in getting students to learn and remember the five French mother sauces (tomato, espagnol, hollandaise, béchamel, velouté)?

A. The five mother sauces are: tomato, velouté, béchamel, hollandaise, and espagnol.

B. BeEs HoVer Too.

C. Tom has ESP, so he knew about the Hall and Oates concert BEfore VEra.

D. There once was a tomato in Spain
Who spent daise and daise without rain
"It's too dry to handle
And I can't be a camel
So I'm left to shrivel out in pain."

E. Béchamel is scalded milk in the roux
Velouté adds veal stock too
Espagnol is brown
Tomato is easily found
And if you've got too many eggs
make them into hollandaise.

Answer: **B.** *BeEs HoVer Too*

It's quick and easy. Bees hover too:

Béchamel
Espagnol
Hollandaise
Velouté
Tomato

As long as you remember it's the pairs of letters that start each sauce, it's a short, logical phrase. No need to overdo it or make a joke.

WRONG ANSWERS

A. *The five mother sauces are: tomato, velouté, béchamel, hollandaise, and espagnol.*

This would be fine, but it's not as effective as B. As a teacher, you should always look for better ways to facilitate learning, like mnemonic devices or wordplay (but not wordplay jokes—I think I might have mentioned that).

C. *Tom has ESP, so he knew about the Hall and Oates concert BEfore VEra.*

This is also a short, funny phrase. The problem with it is the two sauces that are hardest to remember (velouté and béchamel) get crowded in at the end. We don't need to force Hall and Oates in there because, while humorous, people tend to remember well-known sauces like hollandaise.

D. *There once was a tomato in Spain*
Who spent daise and daise without rain
"It's too dry to handle
And I can't be a camel
So I'm left to shrivel out in pain."

This tries too hard. If the first two letters aren't enough to remember béchamel and velouté, asking someone to memorize an entire limerick and then pick out "béchamel" from "be a camel" and "velouté" from "shrivel out" won't help. It would just be easier to do straight memorization. Don't get too cute with your lesson plans: sometimes you just have to bore people and make them memorize stuff if you can't simplify it.

E. *Béchamel is scalded milk in the roux*
Velouté adds veal stock too
Espagnol is brown
Tomato is easily found
And if you've got too many eggs
make them into hollandaise.

First of all, if I'm gonna memorize a whole song verse, it'd better be packed with information. Similar to a student who memorizes 50 prepositions to the tune of "Yankee Doodle Dandy" or something even more remotely useful.

More critically, with the exception of the final line, the rhymes aren't based on the sauces. It's okay for remembering what the sauces are, but if I use this to learn the names, it's going to stick in my memory like this:

Something is scalded milk in the roux
Something else adds veal stock too
Etc.

If you're making up a rhyme, you need the words being memorized to rhyme, or have every single word be part of the list.

Jokemaking Trap 5: Embracing Bad Comedy

"I have a whole bunch of dad jokes," a teacher once proudly confessed to me, "and they always get groans."

That kind of statement twists my mind to the point where I get dizzy, fall down, and cannot get up for several hours.

Maybe there's some alternate universe where students pay attention to poor jokes and hate ice cream and the Tooth Fairy actually exists (but is destitute because of the general hatred for ice cream). But not this universe. I have had a few of those teachers—we all have—and I don't remember anything their poorly constructed jokes were supposed to help me learn. Maybe they weren't supposed to help. Maybe teachers are using bad jokes as a veneer because they are afraid to just teach naturally and be a boring, uncool teacher.

Nah, that couldn't be it. What do I know about comedy, anyway? Nothing, so let me just Google "Why do people tell dumb jokes?"

Weird, most of the first-page results are articles that I've written... Oh, wait, I forgot to search with incognito mode, so Google is just pulling up all the articles where people have told me my jokes are horrible. Great one, Google, I feel burned.

Okay, now let me put incognito mode on and hope to God it's just a way to search anonymously and not a guarantee that every link will be pornography.

Here's a promising blog entry by *Psychology* editor J. Sutton titled "In Defense of Dad Jokes."

> *It just seems natural that I'd want to try to make my kids laugh. The thing is...a lot of my normal material is off limits. Profanity is out. I don't want to make sexual innuendo. I need to be careful about jokes that are biting or sarcastic...I don't want them to see me being mean to others.*
>
> *So where does that leave me? It leaves me with puns. It leaves me with silly jokes... As a dad you want your kids to be surrounded with the warm, happy, innocuous kind of stuff.*
>
> **I think at some level they know that each time they groan or say, "Oh, Dad!" to my admittedly pathetic dad jokes, they're really saying "I love you too."** [21]

The "they-boo-because-they-love-me" ending really undermines the setup.

Here's another source, a Reddit thread with 10,000 upvotes, titled "Dads who tell 'dad jokes' are actually funny people who had to censor their humor for a younger audience."

Okay, so dad jokes are just tools of really, really, gosh-you-gotta-believe-me-I'm-funny comedians whose material was not appropriate for minors. And now they've resorted to telling sophomoric jokes with little to no situational relevance and a heavy dependence on wordplay.

I can work with that.

See, that statement depends on the assumption that there are only two kinds of comedy: inappropriate comedy and goofy wordplay.

A riddle: What does R-rated humor have in common with G-rated, goofy dad jokes?

Answer: They're both lowbrow comedy latched onto by comedians who haven't learned how to properly construct a good situational joke.

It may be harsh, but it's also common sense. It doesn't pass the smell test. "I'm a good comic usually, but I have to tell bad jokes because my audience is young" has all the veracity of "My other wife is a Ferrari."

That's okay, though. The road to comedy is paved with painful revelations. If you want a step-by-step guide on how to construct decent, appropriate jokes, I can't help you.

Just kidding, I can totally help you. That's the point of the previous chapter, so go back and read it more carefully.

QUESTION

All of these jokes are not great and therefore probably won't increase retention except:

A. To a kindergarten class: "Learning the alphabet is as easy as A-B-C."

B. To a 10th-grade algebra class: "If you multiply two numbers with exponents, you add the exponents. Divide two numbers with exponents? Subtract the exponents. If you take one number with an exponent to the power of another exponent, multiply them. Multiply-Add, Divide-Subtract, Power-Multiply. MADSPM. Just remember, 'I gave my email to an exponential number of websites, and now I get Mad Spam.'"

C. To a sixth-grade English class:
"Knock, knock.
Who's there?
To
To who?
It's to whom!"

D. To a first-grade class studying math: "If you have five watermelons in one hand and three watermelons in the other, what do you have? BIG HANDS!"

E. To an eighth-grade English class: "One time, I asked a student to give me a sentence that started with *you*. He said, 'You is,' and I immediately told him, 'Always say *you are* because it's the proper conjugation of *is*.' The student thought for a moment and said, 'Okay. U are the 21st letter of the alphabet.'"

Answer: **B.** *To a 10th-grade algebra class: "If you multiply two numbers with exponents, add the exponents. Divide? Subtract the exponents. If you take one number with an exponent to the power of another exponent, multiply them. Multiply-Add, Divide-Subtract, Power-Multiply. MADSPM. Just remember, 'I gave my email to an exponential number of websites and now I get Mad Spam.'"*

It's succinct and situational. List the exponent rules, group them together, then present a saying that is logical and leads the user to the acronym. The joke derives from the topic (exponents) and the mnemonic (MADSPM).

WRONG ANSWERS

A. *"Learning the alphabet is as easy as A-B-C."*

Foremost, this joke does nothing to help anyone learn the alphabet. It also uses a very common saying, "As easy as A-B-C." Try to avoid that, as clichés can come off as stale, which leads to tuning out. Instead, work something organic and relevant into the comparison, "Learning the alphabet is as easy as screaming, which you will do if you don't learn the alphabet."

C. *"Knock, knock.
Who's there?
To
To who?
It's to whom!"*

You can't have a five-line joke just to associate one preposition with *whom*. That's inefficient. Just say that *whom* follows a preposition, and then make up a fun way to remember prepositions. Or simply go all the way and teach people that it's *whom* when we're referring to the object of the sentence and *who* when it's the subject. It's really not hard to learn if you take a moment to figure out what a subject is (the part of the sentence that is doing the action) versus what the object is (the part of the sentence that is having the action performed upon it).

D. *"If you have five watermelons in one hand and three watermelons in the other, what do you have? BIG HANDS!"*

I fail to see how this popular joke, which was told to me by a first-grade teacher, increases students' ability to figure out what 5 plus 3 is. Perhaps this is where my animosity toward nonconstructive jokes was first conceived, then incubated for 35 years until it emerged a fully formed behemoth of rage. Perhaps not, but I do know that when I tried to do mental math for the next few weeks, my head was overcrowded with watermelons. I can't fit eight watermelons in my head.

E. *"One time, I asked a student to give me a sentence that started with* you. *He said, 'You is,' and I immediately told him, 'Always say* you are *because it's the proper conjugation of* is.' *The student thought for a moment and said, 'Okay. U are the 21st letter of the alphabet.'"*

First, you don't need a paragraph to remind a student that *are* always follows *you*. Second, if someone told me this joke, I would call the police for wordplay crimes. They're cracking down on that.

Jokemaking Trap 6: Monkeycheese

Often, the first type of humor children glom onto is that of silly juxtapositions. When my kids were two years old, their favorite bit was to go back and forth nominating ridiculous pizza toppings: "Bananas!" "Hot dogs!" "Guitars!" Each utterance would be followed by howls of laughter so loud that sometimes they would hit the same pitch frequency, causing my windows to vibrate. Ah, the stuff they never tell you about twins.

However, you can probably see why this isn't a good tool for retention. It specifically relies on doing something *totally unrelated* to the subject matter. This "lol so random" pairing of two unlike things is colloquially referred to as "monkeycheese" humor, and it is very distracting.

Check out these quotes from popular, well-respected educational websites:

I will do almost anything to get the class rolling with laughter— voice inflections, exaggerated facial expressions and movements…
 —NEA.org

That's…not funny. That's just being different.
Let's revisit a quote from earlier:

Teach from the top of your desk, tap dance while you give instructions, speak in an English accent, or sing the answers to a homework assignment. —Miami Herald

Thirteen-year-old me just died from embarrassment.
It's telling that the first quote starts with "I will do almost anything to get the class rolling with laughter," which is in direct contrast to the "pick your spots" mantra of this book. Yeah, don't do this cringeworthy monkeycheese. It comes from a good place: you want the students to focus on you so you can teach. But don't conflate focusing on what you're doing with focusing on what you're teaching.

This may seem intimidating, but it's easy to figure out if what you're doing is focusing or distracting. Does someone tap dancing make you pay more attention to what they're saying? Do newscasters tap dance while reading the news? Can you remember even one line of a Shirley Temple movie? Nope, because tap dancing is distracting.

Does speaking in an English accent make you focus better? No one's ever said, "Hey, this farm report is too boring; let's listen to it on the BBC, and it'll be way easier."

From telegraphing to dancing, if you find yourself tapping to get your message across, you're doing something wrong.

When I debate this with a fellow educator, be it a school principal, yoga instructor, or just someone who likes to condescend a lot, they frequently argue that being "omg totes rando" is a great way to connect with students. Pupils, especially teenage ones, are frequently caught in a stiff web of social constructs and rules. So for a student to see a teacher go beyond the normal boundaries of social expectation builds respect and paints them as a leader.

To this I always respond, "Why do you care so much about what teenagers think of you? That's super sad!" Then I offer to buy the next round as they usually are trying to punch me.

QUESTION

All of these techniques are distracting except:

A. A teacher attempts to quiet a noisy class by standing on her desk and yodeling.

B. A teacher attempts to increase retention for a lesson about post-Civil War reconstruction by delivering the material in a Southern drawl.

C. A teacher arrives at a lesson about marine biology dressed as an octopus.

D. An elementary-school teacher lecturing about insects punches up his lesson by releasing hundreds of angry bees into the classroom.

E. A teacher does the Charleston every time a student's cell phone rings.

Answer: **A.** *A teacher attempts to quiet a noisy class by standing on her desk and yodeling.*

Long ago, humans figured out that loud noises are a great way to get attention. That night, they replaced all the smoke alarms that quietly whispered, "Fire," and never looked back.

By now, you've probably noticed that I was a sarcastic, inattentive student. I was a hard audience; I didn't like "Haha, I'm such a wacky teacher" schemes and techniques because I found them distracting (and not "cool," which was the term for things we thought were "good" back in those days).

The one thing I did like was when a teacher did something weird and loud to get an unruly class's attention. Why? Well, to be honest, I've also had teachers get the class's attention by screaming, "Shut up!" and anything is preferable to that.

Now, don't think I'm basing my advice on what worked on one student, even if that student did grow up to write a best-selling book on teaching with comedy. The effectiveness of using a loud, random noise to quiet discussion has been widely documented by scientists, teaching experts, and sitcom characters.

WRONG ANSWERS

B. *A teacher attempts to increase retention for a lesson about post-Civil War reconstruction by delivering the material in a Southern drawl.*

FUN NOTE: Many teachers have found that using an accent helps increase retention. But there is no evidence that speaking in a funny way helps brains absorb information. What has been shown to work is vocal inflection. When people put on fake accents, they almost always exaggerate their inflections.

Mystery solved! The mystery of "How can we turn these numerous teacher anecdotes around to support my point of view" has been solved. We did it! This was exciting, thanks for sharing the moment with me. Instead of using a fake accent, just make sure your voice isn't monotonous.

C. *A teacher arrives at a lesson about marine biology dressed as an octopus.*

If dressing up doesn't get people's attention, then why did I spend most of my teenage summers wearing a giant book costume and handing out two-for-one drink coupons for the local library?

Because dressing up gets attention, but it doesn't increase retention. If one of my teachers wore an octopus costume, I would become completely distracted with anticipating when one of their rogue arms would accidentally knock something over. Anything they said during this lecture would take forever for me to recall, just like it took forever for me to finally realize that that probably wasn't a real library.

D. *An elementary-school teacher lecturing about insects punches up his lesson by releasing hundreds of angry bees into the classroom.*

This wouldn't increase retention for two subtle reasons. First, your lesson would be difficult to hear over the loud buzzing. Second, the class's attention would be diverted to the bees, as bees are fuzzy and every child wants to pet them.

E. *A teacher does the Charleston every time a student's cell phone rings.*

When I first got into teaching and wanted to incorporate my super-stark brand of humor into my lessons, I did a lot of research on what established teachers claimed would work. This was when I started to suspect that the techniques espoused by experts were less effective than they were reported to be. That's right, my doubts on all of these bogus "teaching tips" I've shared aren't entirely based on my tumultuous emotional childhood. If nothing else, I hope this book has instilled a stronger sense of introspection within you that optimally leads to a greater sense of self-loathing. Your students will appreciate it.

Anyone can claim that students find their "hilarious" dancing and silly voices delightful. Yet when I see claims that it's effective to say something silly or dance when a cell phone rings (a tip I've seen many times), I throw up my arms and loudly exclaim, "HUH?" Because if the dance or voice is so well received, why would you attach it to a bad behavior like leaving a cell phone on? That's rewarding distraction.

There is much to say about showing a human side to gain the trust of a class. When teaching standardized tests, I often highlight when I make a simple mistake and say, "People are under the impression that high scorers make fewer mistakes, to which I say, 'Challenge accepted!'" It's quick, it's droll, it gets a genuine laugh…but not too big a laugh. I'm not trying to impress them with my comedic stylings; I'm trying to make them feel more comfortable about their shortcomings and, let's be honest, move away from the fact I just made a mistake and back to the lesson.

That's important: these students frequently assume people who are good at tests are naturally gifted, and when I show them I'm fallible, it goes a long way toward inspiring them to trust in the methods that got my scores up. When students see a teacher make a mistake, they tend to think, "I thought this guy was supposed to be great, maybe he's not good at all." Pointing out that I make mistakes all the time and still get the test goals they strive for shifts their frame to "Hey, this guy isn't perfect; neither am I, so the stuff he's teaching will probably work for me. Let's stop burning our names into this desk and listen."

It shows I'm human because being imperfect is human. That's situational comedy in a nutshell: use a real situation (making a mistake in front of everyone) to form a joke that keeps student retention high.

You know what doesn't show people you're human? Tap dancing, singing math stuff, or using weird foreign accents (unless you actually are a foreigner).

There's a Philip K. Dick short story I read in high school called "The Hanging Stranger." The main character sees a body hanging from a tree in a busy city area, but no one seems to care. It turns out…spoiler alert…Philip K. Dick was doing a lot of amphetamines. And it also turns out that the hanging body is a signal for body-snatching aliens: those who ignore it are aliens, those who freak out reveal themselves as humans who still need to be body snatched, or probed, or whatever happened at the end of that tale. I kind of forgot (and I bet Philip K. Dick did too).

The point is, weird stuff is alien to a normal student. Never do I question a teacher's humanity more than when they start using bizarre monkeycheese humor in class. It has the opposite of its intended effect. It's distracting.

Right now you are probably saying, "Okay, Evan, I'm totally convinced that monkeycheese is a bad method for teaching older kids, because you have a persuasive and entertaining argumentative style. However, you mentioned your toddlers love it, so why isn't it a great method for increasing retention among younger students?"

To this I reply, "Your flattery is insulting! You need to pay more attention."

I've had my share of experience with children under eight: volunteering at co-op preschools, leading playdates, managing a room full of hyper five-year-olds so all the other parents could take a break and exchange liquor coupons. I even spent a dozen months as an eight-year-old, for research purposes.

While monkeycheese can sometimes lead to a game that successfully corrals the kids, more often than not it will add to the frenetic chaos. For every time I successfully get kids to put away their toys by picking up a toy, yelling out a funny food combination ("This toy airplane with extra mustard"), and putting it away, there have been 10 times where they pick up a toy, yell a funny food combination, howl wildly, yell another food combination even louder, then scream and jump and spin their heads 360 degrees around their necks (that's not just my kids, right?). Instead of monkeycheese, which takes the situation in a random direction, use a 180 to keep things humorous yet structured.

You know what's funnier than a monkey eating cheese?
A zookeeper getting fired for taking bribes from Big Dairy.

Monkeycheese just doesn't work, no matter the age range. Plus, like with puns, like with wordplay, like with filling your lesson with hilarious expletives (I'm sure somebody's tried it), it's not very high effort. Take the time to practice situational humor, and you'll get the retention your well-crafted lesson plans deserve. Plus, situational humor requires a situation, which means you'll be less tempted to insert your well-rehearsed play on words when you don't really need a joke.

Every parent knows the best way to get little kids to clean up is not with a joke, but by telling them it's a game and then occasionally awarding them points for arbitrary reasons.

QUESTION

All of these jokes are situationally relevant in that they appropriately highlight an important point of the lesson except:

A. While teaching creative writing, I underscore how characters are the most important part of every story by stating, "There are a million stories where boy meets girl, but because Shakespeare's characters still resonate with audiences, there's only one *Romeo and Juliet*. Well, also because the characters die at the end, so he couldn't really make a sequel."

B. While teaching the Pythagorean theorem to graduate students, I quip, "This is great for figuring out how much dirt is needed in a right-triangular garden. In college, all of my gardens were right triangular because that was the shape of my dorm-room closet."

C. Trying to explain why a bar graph with bigger bars on the right is actually said to be skewed to the left, I add, "What if you forget that? Do you stand up and scream and throw your test in the air? No, you simply remember that an alternate definition for the word *skew* is 'tail.' It's a really obscure definition because I just made it up, but don't worry about that. Since the graph has a long tail going to the left, it's skewed to the left."

D. Teaching grammar to a bunch of *super-eager* middle-school students, I remark, "A run-on sentence has two or more independent clauses. Why is that bad? Because it's super annoying, as it's a sentence that just goes on without linking together or breaking up. We all hate when our parents are talking to us and go on and on and on. The run-on sentence is the grammar version of your droning parents. So next time you are taking a test and a sentence annoys you, check to see if there is more than one independent clause."

E. Teaching an SAT class, I state, "SAT science passages are always boring. I like science, and they still manage to choose something painfully mundane, like a description of the composition of rocks on Mars. That's good! The details almost never matter in a science passage; it's how they present each paragraph and what the author thinks or supports. So it's actually beneficial that I can't pay attention to extremely stupid rock talk because it frees me up to focus on the structure, which is what most of the questions will be about. Somewhere in this room someone's thinking, 'I like reading about Mars rocks, jerk!' But the one you should really be upset with is the test maker for punishing you for actually knowing about Mars rocks!"

Answer: **C.** *Trying to explain why a bar graph with bigger bars on the right is actually said to be skewed to the left, I add, "What if you forget that? Do you stand up and scream and throw your test in the air? No, you simply remember that an alternate definition for the word* skew *is 'tail.' It's a really obscure definition because I just made it up, but don't worry about that. Since the graph has a long tail going to the left, it's skewed to the left."*

I tried to trick you here, by using a successful technique for dealing with a nervous/low self-esteem student mentioned earlier. It's great for refocusing one student who is letting nerves get the best of them. It's not a situationally relevant way, however, of increasing the retention of an entire class. The farcical outburst has nothing to do with tricks for remembering the skew of a bar graph. In fact, it takes the focus away from bar graphs right before I teach a trick for remembering that it doesn't require humor for classes to remember it.

WRONG ANSWERS

(Don't forget: these weren't the correct answers because they are good executions of various techniques.)

A. *While teaching creative writing, I underscore how characters are the most important part of every story by stating, "There are a million stories where boy meets girl, but because Shakespeare's characters still resonate with audiences, there's only one* Romeo and Juliet. *Well, also because the characters die at the end, so he couldn't really make a sequel."*

Ask a high-school student what makes *Romeo and Juliet* so important, and a lot of times they answer, "Romeo and Juliet die at the end." I want to make sure they realize that's not why the play is so renowned. Now, hopefully, when a student summarizes *Romeo and Juliet*, they'll think back to this "because Shakespeare's characters still resonate with audiences, there's only one *Romeo and Juliet*" line and remember that it's the timelessness of the characters, not how they end up.

B. *While teaching the Pythagorean theorem to graduate students, I quip, "This is great for figuring out how much dirt is needed in a right-triangular garden. In college, all of my gardens were right triangular because that was the shape of my dorm-room closet."*

The key to math, as every teacher and student knows, is to relate it to real life. "When am I ever going to use this?" is a commonly asked question, both in math class and history. Here, I relate it to gardening, using the mirthful image of an indoor-closet garden to create a silly visual. It's the same memorable technique that ushered in huge success for the song "Puff, the Magic Dragon."

D. *Teaching grammar to a bunch of super-eager middle-school students, I remark, "A run-on sentence has two or more independent clauses. Why is that bad? Because it's super annoying, as it's a sentence that just goes on without linking together or breaking up. We all hate when our parents are talking to us and go on and on and on. The run-on sentence is the grammar version of your droning parents. So next time you are taking a test and a sentence annoys you, check to see if there is more than one independent clause."*

The only thing more painful than teaching grammar to middle-schoolers is... well, sometimes I feel like teaching anything to middle-schoolers is maximum on the pain scale. Here, I want to show how parents are annoying not just because middle schoolers can sometimes be frothing cauldrons full of bubbling hormones, but also because sometimes parents use run-on sentences.

E. *Teaching an SAT class, I state, "SAT science passages are always boring. I like science, and they still manage to choose something painfully mundane like a description of the composition of rocks on Mars. That's good! The details almost never matter in a science passage; it's how they present each paragraph and what the author thinks or supports. So it's actually beneficial that I can't pay attention to extremely stupid rock talk because it frees me up to focus on the structure, which is what most of the questions will be about. Somewhere in this room someone's thinking, "I like reading about Mars rocks, jerk!" But the one you should really be upset at is the test maker for punishing you for actually knowing about Mars rocks!"*

Even though I'm telling them something they love to hear (you don't have to understand boring science stuff to ace the science passages on the SAT), they tune out by my fourth sentence about how boring it is. Solution? Whip up a conflict about whether the subject matter actually is boring, then show how even science geniuses can set themselves up for failure if they don't understand the process behind creating the SAT.

Jokemaking Trap 7: Worrying about the Stalwarts

When I was first building up my skills as a Kaplan test-prep teacher, my supervisor gave me some teaching advice that I have found applies just as well to comedy.

I was an okay instructor at first. I was usually rated 8 out of 10 by students, with a few higher scores and a few really bad scores. I mean really bad scores: 1s and 2s with notes attached like, "This instructor focuses too much on tricks and not enough on making me learn all the hard math," "This instructor seems nervous and tries to be funny too often," "I would rather go back to the eunuch UFO cult I escaped as a child than learn from this guy," etc. Obviously, I was greatly concerned with that. I wanted it to stop.

So when my boss called me in to my semi-annual performance review, I came prepared with a notebook full of ideas on how to give those 1s and 2s a more satisfying educational experience. About five minutes into me detailing my ideas, he stopped me and said:

> Don't worry about the 1s and 2s. For all you know, those students would hate the class no matter what you do. Maybe they hate the subject. Maybe they are scared to put any responsibility for success on themselves. Maybe they're just weird. You don't want to be spending an inordinate amount of time focusing on someone who just won't enjoy the process no matter what.
>
> Instead, focus on the 8s. Those people clearly have the potential to improve, and they are having a good time learning the material, so it should be possible to turn that good time into a great one.

That was the key to me turning my streak of 8s into a streak of perfect scores from happy customers who got the test score improvements they wanted and had a good time doing it.

Also, the 1 and 2 reviews stopped. I don't know why for sure, but I can speculate. Maybe it's because improving the general outlook of the whole class improved the attitudes of even the biggest stalwarts. Maybe the attitudes of the low-raters didn't improve, but the increased enthusiasm of the class made them doubt that the reason for their malaise was because of me. Or maybe they just hated being called on during class, and so my shift in attention to the enthusiastic students brought them some reprieve.

Whatever it was, there is definitely a precedent for this in comedy. When a comic is doing a set on stage, and someone who is having a horrible time heckles them, what do they do? Do they say, "Let me try to tell some jokes that might appeal to you more; let me focus on making you laugh?" Never. Instead, they verbally spar with the heckler, not to make them laugh, but to make the audience that already likes their jokes laugh even harder. To turn those 8s into 9s and 10s.

Now, naturally, I'm not advocating that you seek out your students who are having a horrible time and insult them. Seriously, don't do that (and if you do, don't blame me for it). I'm simply trying to illustrate that focusing on those that are having an enjoyable time is a key for many outlets of public speaking.

QUESTION

Not everything at Colonel Zoron's mutant academy is exciting. Your teenage-level accounting class is proof of that. During a difficult lesson about compound interest, you call on budding mutant Steven Corson, whose superpower is that he can read hundreds of Facebook posts without ever blocking any of his relatives. Frustrated, Corson retorts, "Compound interest is stupid. I'm just going to turn bad and rob banks rather than use it." The class buzzes, and this time it's not just Zach "Bee Boy" Jenner. What's the best joke to prevent your class from becoming the origin story for a supervillain?

A. "Your evil compound sounds interesting, but it won't get you compound interest!"

B. "With the way banks are operating these days, that would probably make you a good guy!"

C. "That might work. Can anyone find a solution to the problem without committing a felony?"

D. "Shark Girl, isn't your dad president of a bank? How does Steven's comment make you feel?"

E. "That's a great idea! Especially the part where you told us all ahead of time so we can stop you!"

Answer: **C.** *"That might work. Can anyone find a solution to the problem without committing a felony?"*

Acknowledge it neutrally, then take the focus away from the student with a situationally relevant quip. We all know the deal with jokers—they want attention. I know I did when I was in high school (it wasn't a mutant high school; I was just really weird). Don't empower him with a direct response; don't try to sell him on the value of learning the compound-interest formula. Instead, focus on the students who want to solve the problem.

WRONG ANSWERS

A. *"Your evil compound sounds interesting, but it won't get you compound interest!"*

As much as I hate wordplay, I don't really hate this. It's kind of cute. It could be because it rearranges two words to create a new meaning, but more likely I think it's cute because I wrote it and can't get over ego bias.

Questions of merit aside, it's not a great way to dissolve the tension for a couple of reasons. First, you're not really making an argument. Steven knows he won't get compound interest from stacking a bunch of money in his evil lair. Also, it doesn't really shift the focus toward solving the problem. Even if it wins over Steven, you're still at the point where a student who cannot or will not figure out the problem has the floor.

B. *"With the way banks are operating these days, that would probably make you a good guy!"*

This is a funny retort, but it falls into the number one don't of this entire book: don't make a joke just to be funny. This joke doesn't focus the discussion back on the lesson, and it doesn't dismiss the student's sarcasm. In fact, it calls further attention to it. Also, this joke is a bit politically charged, which we want to avoid.

D. *"Shark Girl, isn't your dad president of a bank? How does Steven's comment make you feel?"*

This is pretty low—passing the ire from you to another student. Schlemiel-schlimazel is for revitalizing a distracted, sleepy class, not for throwing a student under the bus so you don't have to face a heckler.

E. *"That's a great idea! Especially the part where you told us all ahead of time so we can stop you!"*

This kind of negative attention is exactly what the sarcastic student wants. It's also unnecessarily aggressive. I'm sure you all know this, but once you get in an argument with a smart-aleck student, you've already lost.

There you have it: the seven traps that could foil your quest for more attentive students. Even if your first reaction is, "Hey, I've been doing these for years, and my classes seem fine," deep in your heart you know your oration could stand a bit of improvement. Because, after all, you did just complete a workbook on how to improve your comedy as a teacher.

CONCLUSION

We have come to the end of the book. Like most authors, I will now give you my home address so, if you have any questions, you can come over and bother me.

I hope that the self-reflection you no doubt underwent when I called out ineffective types of humor wasn't too painful.

Most of all, I hope this helps your students get more interested in learning. Nothing is more arduous than having to lecture to students who aren't learning, whether they're kindergarteners who are too wound up or Saturday-morning SAT students whose parents forced them to be there. I've struggled through a wide range of these difficult situations, and it still amazes me how attention spans can be turned on if I'm putting on an entertaining show that focuses primarily on the lesson.

It also amazes me how fast students' attention flips off if I'm making too many jokes or delivering a bit about something they just can't relate to. That's the original reason I came up with this book idea. I don't think a lot of teachers want to admit that their delivery and material are making their classes learn less, not more, but a little introspection is worth it if student retention shoots up.

Finally, thank you for being a teacher. It's an overworked, underpaid job that sees constant struggles. Every year, you all have to start over with winning the attention of brand-new classes. Thank you; you make the world happen. I hope this book has brought some joy into your life.

I'm always looking to learn more. So if you see me in the street, come on over and let's talk about teaching. Seriously, I'm not in the educational self-help book industry for the money…

I'm in it for the attention.

—Evan Hoovler

ENDNOTES

1. Plato, *Republic*, 360e–361b.
2. Plato, *The Philebus of Plato*, 48–50.
3. Plato, *Laws*, 816e.
4. Melissa B. Wanzer, Ann B. Frymier, and Jeffrey Irwin, "An Explanation of the Relationship between Instructor Humor and Student Learning: Instructional Humor Processing Theory," *Communication Education*, 59 no. 1 (2010): 1–18, DOI: 10.1080/03634520903367238.
5. R. McNeely, "Using Humor in the Classroom." Retrieved May 15, 2019 from http://www.nea.org/tools/52165.htm.
6. Francis MacDonald Cornford, *The Origin of Attic Comedy* (Cambridge: University Press, 1934), 3–4.
7. Aristotle, *Aristotle's Poetics*, trans. S.H. Butcher (New York, NY: Hill and Wang, 1961), 1449a.
8. P. Desberg, et al., "The Effect of Humor on Retention of Lecture Material," presented at a meeting of the American Psychological Association, Montreal, 2016, 1–7. Retrieved from citeseerx.ist.psu.edu/viewdoc/downloaddoi=10.1.1.851.7142&rep=rep1&type=pdf.
9. Ibid.
10. D. Zillmann, et al., "Acquisition of Information from Educational Television Programs as a Function of Differently Paced Humorous Inserts," *Journal of Educational Psychology*, 72 no. 2 (May 1980): 170–180.
11. Simon Newman, "Education in the Middle Ages," accessed May 15, 2019, www.thefinertimes.com.
12. "Public Knowledge of Current Affairs Little Changed by News and Information Revolutions: What Americans Know: 1989–2007," Pew Research Center, April 15, 2007, www.people-press.org.
13. M. Lovorn, "Humor in the Home and in the Classroom: The Benefits of Laughing While We Learn," *Journal of Education and Human Development*, 2 no. 1, 2008.
14. Ibid.
15. Ibid.
16. Joseph Manca, "George Washington's Use of Humor During the Revolutionary War," *Journal of the American Revolution*, February 5, 2015, allthingsliberty.com/2015/02/george-washingtons-use-of-humor-during-the-revolutionary-war.
17. "Kinds of Comedy in Diverse Historical Periods," *Encyclopædia Britannica*, accessed May 15, 2019, www.britannica.com (see, not all my sources are Wikipedia—I use other sketchy online encyclopedias too).

18 Mark Twain, *Innocents Abroad* (1869).
19 S.V. Hellman, "Humor in the Classroom: Stu's Seven Simple Steps to Success," *College Teaching*, 55 no. 1 (2007): 37–39.
20 D. Paquette, "Even the Most Empowered Girls Are More Anxious about Math than Boys," *Washington Post*, May 5, 2016, www.washingtonpost.com/news/wonk/wp/2016/05/05/the-victims-of-math-anxiety/.
21 J. Sutton. "Dad Jokes and the Psychology of Humour." *Dad Pride*, March 5, 2013. Retrieved from http://dadpride.blogspot.com/2013/03/dad-jokes-and-psychology-of-humour.html.

ART CREDITS

Rob Austin (112)
Robert@robertaustindesign.com

Kevin Fleeman (88)
www.artstation.com/kevinfleeman

Annie Hoovler (17)
facebook.com/evan.hoovler

Brad Kohlenberg (3, 6, 31)
@bradkohl

Cynthia Mar (45, 75)
www.instagram.com/cynesthesiaart/

Chris MacDougall (33, 57, 85)
www.instagram.com/mackelangelo/

Sarah McClelland (36, 136, 137)
@missarahbunny

Matthew Sparks (107)
contactus@micromodelsusa.com

George Ward (9, 92)
@burnstyle

Scott Winget (124, 132)
@ScottWinget_CO

Special thanks to Rainier Growlers for artistic inspiration.

www.ingramcontent.com/pod-product-compliance
Lightning Source LLC
LaVergne TN
LVHW051604070426
835507LV00021B/2752